TEACH YOURSELF
PALAEOGRAPHY

A GUIDE FOR GENEALOGISTS AND LOCAL HISTORIANS

CLAIRE JARVIS

First published 2022

The History Press
97 St George's Place, Cheltenham,
Gloucestershire, GL50 3QB
www.thehistorypress.co.uk

British Library Cataloguing in Publication Data.
A catalogue record for this book is available from the British Library.

ISBN 978 0 7509 9877 2

Typesetting and origination by The History Press
Printed and bound in Great Britain by TJ Books Limited, Padstow, Cornwall.

Trees for Life

Contents

Acknowledgements

My thanks are due to the following for their kind permission to reproduce the images in this book:

Derbyshire Record Office
Dorset History Centre
Essex Record Office
Gloucestershire Archives
London Metropolitan Archives
Surrey History Centre
The National Archives
Warwickshire County Record Office
West Yorkshire Archive Service
Wiltshire and Swindon History Centre

I owe an endless debt of gratitude to Adrian Spencer Jarvis (1966–2015), and this book is dedicated to his memory. *Dis aliter visum.*

Introduction

Have you ever searched a nineteenth-century census for a name you are sure must be there but is unaccountably missing? A simple thirty-second search stretches into an afternoon as you digitally search the streets, house by house, for your elusive ancestors, only to find that they have been mistranscribed in the online index used to search the records and appear under a different name altogether.

It shouldn't happen: nineteenth-century handwriting is easy to read with a little practice. A transcription error for one of my own ancestors, of Heuman for Henman, shown in Figure 1, would have been avoided if the indexer had made a careful comparison of similar letter forms on the same page, and was perhaps familiar with common English surnames. (The online indexes referred to throughout are those provided by Ancestry; similar transcription errors occur in the indexes of all family history websites.)

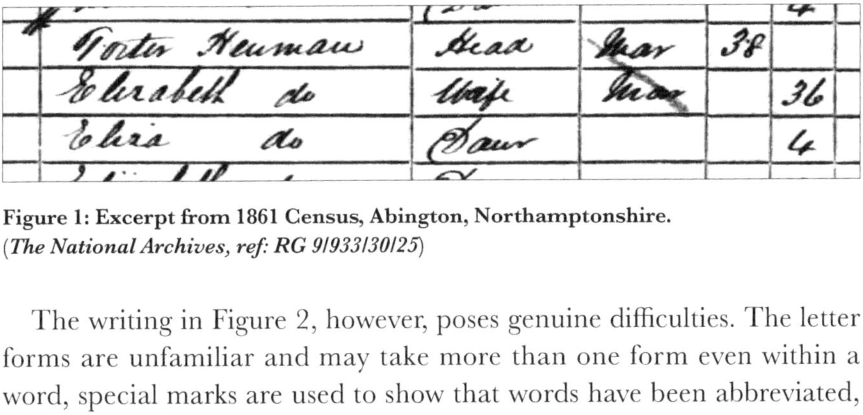

Figure 1: Excerpt from 1861 Census, Abington, Northamptonshire.
(*The National Archives, ref: RG 9/933/30/25*)

The writing in Figure 2, however, poses genuine difficulties. The letter forms are unfamiliar and may take more than one form even within a word, special marks are used to show that words have been abbreviated, and common English forenames have been written in Latin. Furthermore, the ink has bled through the paper from the following page in the original document, making the writing difficult to decipher. It is simply not possible to read this without some training. In this case, 'William Ashewell, son of John Ashewell' was transcribed in the online index as 'Willms Atherwett son of Chois Atherwett', and wrongly dated 1570 instead of 1544.

Transcription errors are not always a problem; the online search uses an algorithm to generate alternative spellings of names, and in the case of my Northamptonshire ancestor, Heuman was indeed matched as a possible alternative to Henman. Unsurprisingly, however, the name Atherwett does not appear as a possible match for Ashwell, and I might well have assumed that that this Surrey ancestor did not appear in the parish register. (In fact, at least half of all the entries in the Latin part of this sixteenth-century register are mistranscribed, making the online index almost useless. Many are serious errors that will not be matched as alternative spellings of names: for example, Sanrans for Laurans, Wyeahel for Nycholus, or Sanpyn for Turpyn.) It is possible to read sixteenth-century handwriting as easily as nineteenth-century handwriting with practice, and a quick scan of the register showed a number of Ashwells resident in sixteenth-century Kingston.

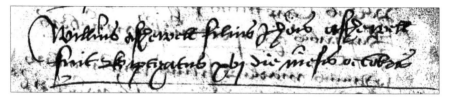

Figure 2: Excerpt from parish register, All Saints, Kingston upon Thames, Surrey, 16 October 1544. (*Surrey History Centre, ref: P33/1/1*)

Transcription:
> *Willi[elm]us ashewell filius Jho[ann]is ashewell*
> *fuit Baptizatus xvi die me[n]sis octobris*

Translation:
> *William Ashwell son of John Ashwell*
> *was baptised on the sixteenth day of the month of October*

Many records in local archives, however, ranging from nineteenth-century poor law records to seventeenth-century quarter sessions records, and from sixteenth-century manor court rolls to twelfth-century charters, and an ever-increasing volume of digital images, are not indexed at all. If you want to read them, you'll have to do it yourself.

I had two aims in mind when I started this book. The first was to provide the sort of guide that I needed when I started researching population history at Cambridge University as a post-graduate many years ago. I found that it was easy enough with a little practice to read eighteenth-century parish registers, but I quickly ran into difficulties with court records from the same date, which were sometimes in Latin, and often written in a bewilderingly difficult script. I could pick my way through a neat fourteenth-century deed, but found manor court rolls of the same date, with their abundance of impenetrable abbreviations, completely inaccessible.

This, then, is the 'teach yourself' book that would have been useful to me, a manual for learning to read old handwriting. If you follow it from beginning to end, you should be able to tackle any record that might be found at any date in English archives. It should be useful, both for the beginner starting out on original documents for the first time, and for the more experienced researcher who, having painstakingly constructed a family tree, now wishes to get to grips with the abundance of records that add context to their personal histories.

My second aim is to provide a one-stop reference guide to all the different letter forms, symbols and abbreviations that have been used in English records over time. This pulls together information from the wide range of publications that I have acquired over the years, many out of print, each covering one particular aspect of old handwriting, such as Tudor secretary hand, medieval court hands, or Latin abbreviations and symbols, and has been informed by years of experience transcribing and translating a wide variety of historical records.

It is important to also say what this book is not. It is not a course in Latin; most records from the early eighteenth century, and many interesting records from earlier centuries, were written in English, and it is possible to undertake a good deal of useful research without any Latin at all. Much of the book is concerned with records written in English, and the Latin documents can be passed over if they are not of interest.

However, the serious genealogist will undoubtedly wish at some time to make use of documents written in Latin. Some records, such as parish registers and the probate clauses of wills, are accessible with a rudimentary knowledge of Latin, but others – in particular, the records of the various courts of law – require a good working knowledge of the language. It will be sufficient to work through the indispensable *Latin for Local History* by Eileen A. Gooder before attempting to read the documents in Latin in this book.

This book is also not, despite the title, concerned with the academic discipline of palaeography, which covers all aspects of the reading, dating, development and classification of handwriting in documents and manuscripts. This book is for the researcher who has a practical need to read old handwriting, with the sole aim of accessing the textual content of records.

Genealogists by necessity generally work backwards in time from known events, and this book works in the same way, taking you from the nineteenth century in easy stages to the medieval period, focusing on records that are of particular interest to the family historian. The five chapters of the book work backwards in time, from the modern, legible handwriting of the past 250 years, back through the round and italic hands of the seventeenth century, to the mixed and secretary hands of the sixteenth century, and the medieval set and other court hands used in public and legal records.

There are some disadvantages to working backwards in time to examine handwriting. Letter forms from earlier times persist in handwriting long after new scripts are generally current, meaning that a knowledge of earlier letter forms is always necessary. Indeed, according to the archivist Hilary Jenkinson, students proposing to work on sixteenth-century writings should start their preparation at a development no later than Domesday, and preferably with the Caroline minuscule!

Also, counter-intuitively, it is often the case that earlier records are easier to read than their later counterparts. We shall see in Chapter 4 that Elizabethan handwriting is often more difficult to read than early Tudor and late medieval handwriting. We shall also see, in Chapter 5, that the highly stylised court handwriting of the early eighteenth century means that public records from that date are considerably harder to read than those of the fifteenth century and before. Accordingly, early letter forms are introduced where necessary, so by the end of the book you should not only be able to work backwards to read the documents of any chosen date, but also have a basic understanding of the development of English documentary handwriting over five centuries.

There is nothing inherently difficult about reading old handwriting. As the palaeographer L.C. Hector pointed out, the reading of manuscripts is not so much about the application of theoretical knowledge, but the exercise of a skill requiring effort on the part of the learner, and a good deal of patient practice. This is not always easy to do, as transcripts of original documents are necessary for checking the accuracy of practice work.

This book provides a series of exercises in transcription with model answers; and further practice is suggested from the huge variety of documents available online, at local record offices, or at The National Archives. Each chapter ends with a selection of excerpts from documents of particular interest to genealogists, exemplifying the key features of the handwriting of the period.

Before you start, it might be useful to read through Appendix A, which provides a glossary of terms used in the book, notes on documentary hands and introduces some commonly used handwriting terminology.

Model transcriptions for all exercises are given towards the end of the book after the final chapter.

1. The Nineteenth and Eighteenth Centuries

- Introduction to transcription
- Letters that take more than one form
- Abbreviations used in documents written in English
- Unfamiliar words and idiosyncratic spellings

This chapter covers handwriting from the late nineteenth century back to the mid-eighteenth century. In 1733, Acts of Parliament came into force that made English rather than Latin the language of the written records of the courts of England. This put an end to the use of highly abbreviated Latin, and the handwriting commonly called 'court hand'. From this date, letter forms are recognisably modern, and can mostly be read with a knowledge of modern scripts alone.

EXERCISE 1.1

The later nineteenth-century censuses are a good starting point for learning to read eighteenth and nineteenth-century hands with ease. Local archives and local studies libraries generally provide free access to the family history websites Ancestry and Findmypast, which both include all the available British census records in their record sets. Browse the 1891 England census online, select an enumeration district for any civil parish of interest, and begin by copying out the description of the district written by the enumerator. This will give practice reading continuous prose, with the added advantage that the descriptions will also contain several initial capital letters used for proper names.

Move on to the first page of the enumeration book, and, with the online index hidden, copy out a whole page. If there are any difficulties with a name or occupation, check each letter carefully against letters in other names or words on the page that you are sure about.

Repeat the exercise for earlier censuses and other enumeration districts, ending with a page from one of the civil parishes in the Middlesex census of 1841, such as St Andrew Holborn or St Mary Whitechapel, which contain a wide variety of occupations and foreign names.

EXERCISE 1.2

Read Appendix B, Transcription Conventions, and, following the guidelines for semi-diplomatic transcription, transcribe the enumerator's description shown in Figure 1.1. Census Enumerators' Books are only available to view online, and the quality of the image may be poor, as it is here, adding to difficulties with legibility. Note that the small letter 'r' takes two different forms; and there is a rather idiosyncratic capital letter 'W'.

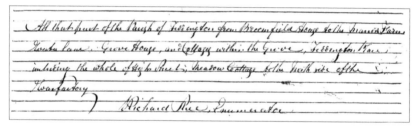

Figure 1.1: Census enumerator's description, Enumeration District 3a, Teddington, Middlesex, 1851 Census. (*The National Archives, ref: HO 107/1604/355*)

EXERCISE 1.3

Browse any enumeration district of interest and, with the online index shown, select unfamiliar and unlikely names for checking and correcting. For example, the name in the last line of Figure 1.2 was mistranscribed in the online index to the 1871 census as Stephen Sicense. Checking the first letter of the surname against the forename and occupation shows that this writer joined his capital 'L' to the next letter but did not do so with a capital 'S'. The name, correctly transcribed, is Stephen License.

The name in the first line of Figure 1.2 was also mistranscribed. Again, a quick check of capital letters elsewhere on the page shows that Benjamin Sirman should in fact be Benjamin Firman.

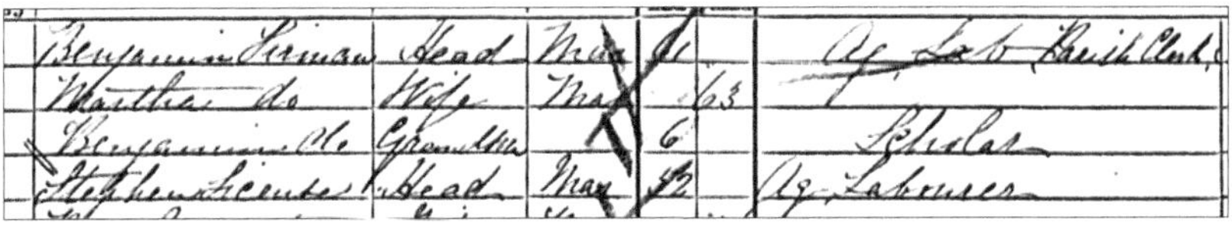

Figure 1.2: Census Enumerator's Book, Palgrave, Suffolk, 1871 Census. (*The National Archives, ref: RG 10/1736/68/15*)

Not all unlikely or unfamiliar names will be incorrect in the online indexes, but most will be. In a quick survey of the online index for a couple of pages of the 1871 Teddington, Middlesex, census, for example, I found Conseline for Cornelius, Remp for Kemp, Lu James for Sir James, and Mbrook for Fullbrook.

EXERCISE 1.4

Transcribe the following excerpt from a contemporary transcript of a baptism register, which introduces the long form 's', which is often mistaken for an 'f', and one possibly unfamiliar term. This exercise also introduces some very common abbreviations that are still used today: a raised final letter, indicating that earlier letters have been omitted; a point or comma, indicating that the word has been abbreviated; and the use of the ampersand representing the word 'and'.

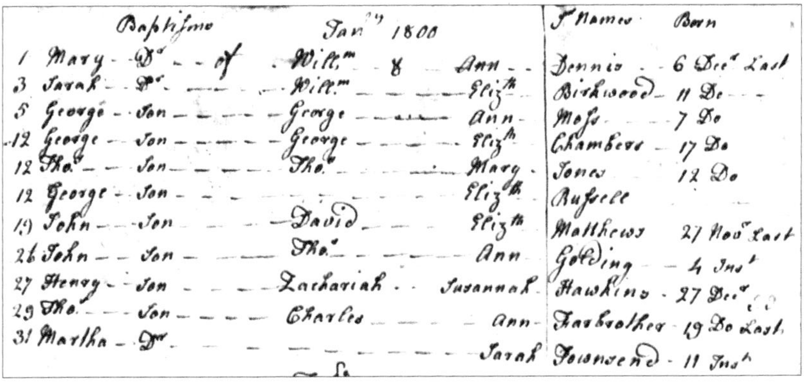

Baptisms		Jan^ry 1800		Sr Names	Born
1 Mary	D^o of	Willm &	Ann	Dennis	6 Decr Last
3 Sarah	D^o	Willm	Eliz^th	Birkwood	11 D^o
5 George	Son	George	Ann	Moss	7 D^o
12 George	Son	George	Eliz^th	Chambers	17 D^o
12 Thos	Son	Thos	Mary	Jones	12 D^o
12 George	Son		Eliz^th	Russell	
19 John	Son	David	Eliz^th	Matthews	27 Novr Last
26 John	Son	Thos	Ann	Golding	4 Ins^t
27 Henry	Son	Zachariah	Susannah	Hawkins	27 Dec^r
29 Thos	Son	Charles	Ann	Farbrother	19 D^o Last
31 Martha	D^r		Sarah	Townsend	11 Ins^t

Figure 1.3: Baptisms, Bishop's Transcript, All Saints, Kingston upon Thames, Surrey, 1800. (*London Metropolitan Archives, City of London, ref: DW/T/6093. Reproduced by kind permission of the Diocese of Winchester*)

EXERCISE 1.5

Transcribe the following lines from a mid-eighteenth-century Gloucestershire probate inventory. Note the use of the reverse 'e', the only letter form that is not italic; both the long and short form of the small letter 's'; and the Saxon 'thorn', which was frequently used to represent the letters 'th' and is indistinguishable here from the letter 'y', that appears in line 2 (see Appendix D: Marks of Abbreviation in English).

The only difficulties likely to arise are those caused by phonetic spelling ('imnetary' for 'inventory' in line 1, and 'acer' for 'acre' in line 8), and the use of unfamiliar words (the sixth word of line 7), or of words that have different meanings today ('praised' in line 9).

Figure 1.4: **Probate Inventory, Bitton, Gloucestershire, 1752.** (*Gloucestershire Archives, ref: GDR/Inv/1752/34 ILES William*)

EXERCISE 1.6

Before attempting the following exercise, spend some time transcribing some of the Poor Law Removal and Settlement records available online, which will provide practice reading both lists of names (for example, Orders of Removal and Birth Books), and pages of continuous text (Settlement Papers). The records in the Shoreditch Union Book of Examinations in Ancestry's London Poor Law Removal and Settlement Records, 1698–1930, are particularly useful. Although the letter forms are italic, and therefore easily recognisable, the entries are not particularly easy to read, with several words abbreviated with a point and a raised final letter (which may or may not be the final letter of the word):

Figure 1.5: Excerpts from eighteenth-century settlement examinations.

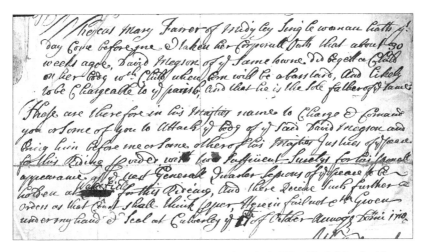

a. Conveyance Order, Midgley, West Yorkshire, 1718. (*West Yorkshire Archive Service, ref: MISC 5/96a/23*)

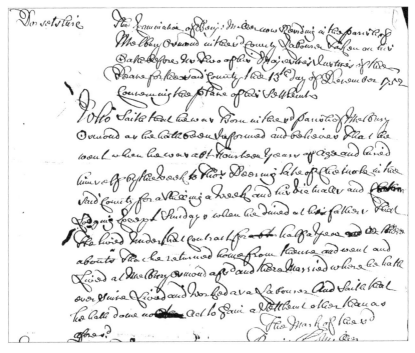

b. Settlement Examination, Melbury Osmond, Dorset, 1752. (*Dorset History Centre, ref: PE/MBO: OV 4/2/2*)

Final Selections: Excerpts from Eighteenth and Nineteenth-Century Records

EXERCISE 1.7

The letter forms in the first excerpt in the final selection of eighteenth and nineteenth-century records are mostly recognisably modern, apart from the long-form 's', reverse 'e', and a new letter form, the right-angle 'c'.

The census enumerator's description (excerpt b) from a century later, however, is much more difficult to read: note that the 'a' is open-top, and identical to 'u', and that the 'v' is similar to the 'r'. The original will (excerpt d) introduces the three-form superior 'r'.

Spelling in the final probate inventory (excerpt f) is highly phonetic but should not cause problems; note, in particular, a phrase commonly used in inventories, 'wearing apparel and money in purse'.

Figure 1.6: Excerpts from eighteenth and nineteenth-century records.

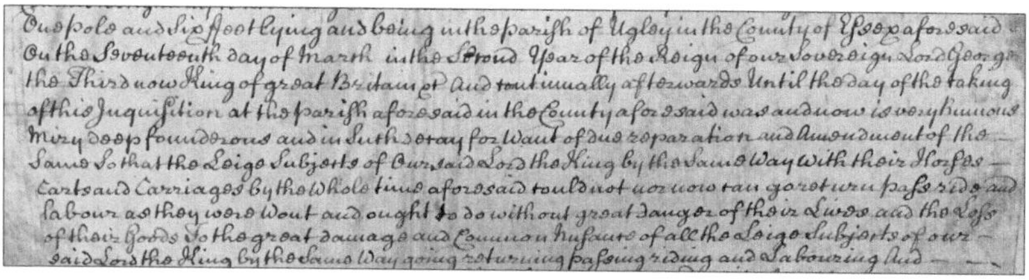
One pole and Six feet lying and being in the parish of Ugley in the County of Essex aforesaid
On the Seventeenth day of March in the Second Year of the Reign of our Sovereign Lord George
the Third now King of great Britain &c And continually afterwards Until the day of the taking
of this Inquisition at the parish aforesaid in the County aforesaid was and now is very ruinous
miry deep founderous and in Such decay for Want of due reparation and Amendment of the
Same So that the Liege Subjects of Our said Lord the King by the Same Way with their Horses
Carts and Carriages by the Whole time aforesaid could not nor now can go return pass ride and
labour as they were Wont and ought to do without great danger of their Lives and the Loss
of their Goods To the great damage and Common Nusance of all the Liege Subjects of our
said Lord the King by the Same Way going returning passing riding and Labouring And

a. Inquisition, Ugley, Essex, 1762. (***Norfolk and Home Circuits Assizes Indictment File, The National Archives, ref: ASSI 94/959***)

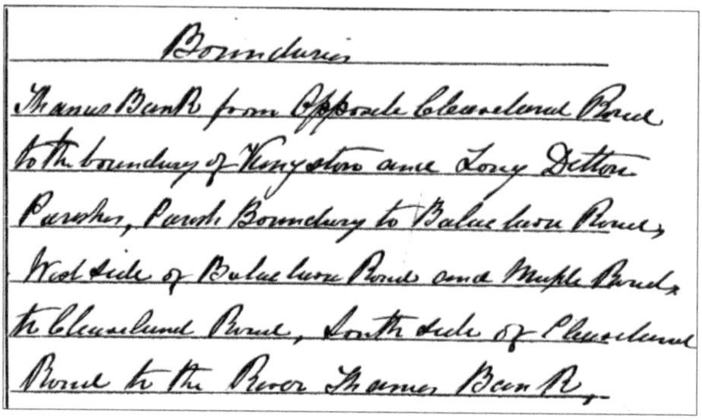
Boundaries
Thames Bank from Opposite Cleaveland Road
to the boundary of Kingston and Long Ditton
Parishes, Parish Boundary to Balaclava Road,
West side of Balaclava Road and Maple Road,
to Cleaveland Road, South side of Cleaveland
Road to the River Thames Bank,

b. Census Enumerator's Description, Enumeration District 21, Kingston Upon Thames, Surrey, 1881 Census. (***The National Archives, ref: RG 11/836/79***)

c. Baptisms, Parish Register, Bream, Gloucestershire, 1785.
(*Gloucestershire Archives, ref: P57/IN/1/1*)

d. Will of William Barnes, Horley, Surrey, 1730. (*London Metropolitan Archives, City of London, ref: DW/PA/05/1730/009. Reproduced by kind permission of the Diocese of Winchester*)

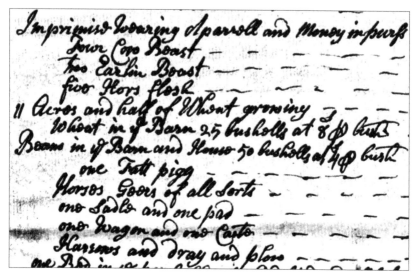

e. Probate Inventory, Westbury on Severn, Gloucestershire, 1776.
(*Gloucestershire Archives, ref: GDR/Inv/1776/11 BELLAMY William*)

f. Probate Inventory, Horsley, Gloucestershire, 1735. (*Gloucestershire Archives, ref: GDR/Inv/1735/23 DAVIS Samuel*)

Further Practice and Resources for Reading Eighteenth and Nineteenth-Century Hands

There are a few plates of eighteenth-century documents with model transcriptions in both Hilda Grieve's *Examples of English Handwriting 1150–1750* and Hilary Marshall's *Palaeography for Family and Local Historians*, and it is worth making your own transcriptions of these and correcting any errors you make. There are also some excellent transcripts of parish registers that may similarly be used to check and correct your own efforts; compare, for example, your own transcription of a late eighteenth-century London parish register, such as St Martin Outwich (available to view online at Ancestry) with Bruce Bannerman's transcript, which is available in the library of The National Archives.

Probate records are a particularly good source for reading practice. Large numbers of wills are available to view online, and a familiarity with the form, structure and wording of eighteenth and nineteenth-century records will provide a firm basis for reading earlier wills in English and Latin.

Some probate inventories may be found online, and most local records offices hold large numbers of them. They provide an invaluable introduction to deciphering unfamiliar words. Stuart A. Raymond's *Words from Wills and Other Probate Records 1500–1800*, and Joy Bristow's *The Local Historian's Glossary of Words and Terms* between them will cover most words encountered; as with wills, plenty of practice reading eighteenth-century records will mean that sixteenth-century inventories do not come as too much of a shock.

2. The Later Seventeenth Century

- Secretary letter forms in mixed hands
- Further abbreviations in English
- Dates
- Introduction to documents written in Latin

This chapter examines handwriting from the middle of the seventeenth century, which mixes 'secretary' letter forms with later italic letter forms and introduces seventeenth-century records written in these mixed hands in Latin. Tudor secretary had emerged from earlier court hands as a distinctive hand in the sixteenth century and was primarily used for writing business and administrative records at speed in English. Although secretary hand had been displaced by later scripts by the mid-seventeenth century, some letter forms persisted well into the late seventeenth century.

EXERCISE 2.1

In the eighteenth century, it is common to find that letters take more than one form, but they are generally recognisably modern. The following seventeenth-century hand, however, although mainly italic, retains many characteristics of secretary hand, and contains several unfamiliar letter forms. As you transcribe the late seventeenth-century juror's list shown in Figure 2.1, note the following, all taken from the same list:

The right-angle 'c' and the x-form of the letter 'p' and in the word 'coppy', and the twin-stemmed 'r' and reverse 'e' in 'true':

The two-stroke 'e', occasionally used instead of the reverse 'e', both used here in the word 'there', and the non-bodied form of 'h' in 'w[i]thin':

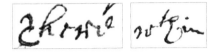

In addition, as well as italic 's', the long form is used medially, and sigma 's' is used terminally.

There are also two common abbreviations here, a loop back and through the descender of the letter 'p' indicating an abbreviation for 'per' or 'par', and the extension upward and backward of a terminal letter as a general mark of suspension.

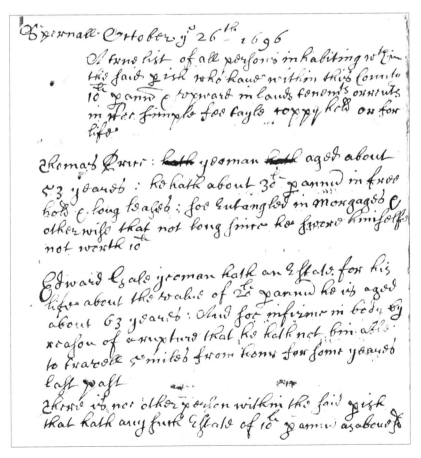

Figure 2.1: Jurors' list, Spernall, Warwickshire, 1696.
(*Warwickshire County Record Office, ref: QS 76/33*)

A digital image of this document, and similar records, may be viewed online on Ancestry in the Warwickshire, England, Occupational and Quarter Sessions Records, 1662–1866 collection. Jurors' Lists are particularly useful, as they contain text as well as lists of names written in the same hand, giving scope for the comparison of unfamiliar letters. Spend plenty of time transcribing pages from the Jurors' Lists of 1696 and 1704, referring to the secretary alphabet in Appendix C.1 if necessary.

EXERCISE 2.2

The following exercise covers the capital letters that often cause some difficulty, as secretary (and court) capitals persisted in mixed hands well into the eighteenth century. Once they have been mastered, the thousands of names in the Hearth Tax records, also available online on Ancestry in the Warwickshire Occupational and Quarter Sessions Records, should present no problems. All the examples here are taken from late seventeenth-century records and mix secretary and italic letter forms.

Figure 2.2: Selected names from late seventeenth-century records.

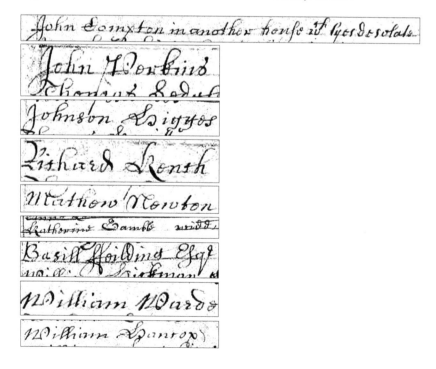

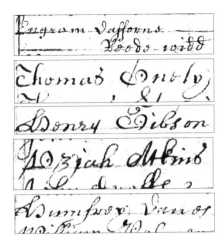

Hearth Tax returns, Knightlow Hundred, Warwickshire, 1662. (*Warwickshire County Record Office, ref: QS 11/1*)

Apprenticeship Bond, St Andrew, Enfield, 1695. (*London Metropolitan Archives, City of London, ref: DRO/004/A/07/002. Reproduced by kind permission of the Parish of St Andrew, Enfield*)

EXERCISE 2.3

Referring to Appendix D.1: Marks of Abbreviation: English, tackle the following exercise, which covers all of the remaining abbreviations likely to be found in seventeenth-century documents written in English.

Figure 2.3: Examples of common abbreviations in English documents in the late seventeenth and early eighteenth centuries.

a. Settlement certificate, St Andrew, Enfield, 1699. (*London Metropolitan Archives, City of London, ref: DRO/004/D/03/001. Reproduced by kind permission of the Parish of St Andrew, Enfield*)

b. Condition of Bastardy Bond, St Andrew, Enfield, 1704. (*London Metropolitan Archives, City of London, ref: DRO/004/D/06/002. Reproduced by kind permission of the Parish of St Andrew, Enfield*)

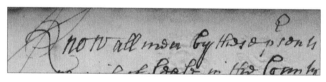

c. Testimonial Letter, Navy Board In-Letters, 1676. (*The National Archives, ref: ADM 106/322/30*)

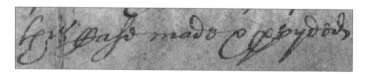

d. Apprenticeship bond, St Peter Cornhill, London, 1700. (*London Metropolitan Archives, City of London, ref: P69/PET1/B/033/MS0420. Reproduced by kind permission of the Parish of St Helen, Bishopsgate*)

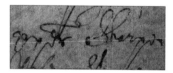

e. Bill of Indictment, Middlesex Sessions of the Peace, 1651. (*London Metropolitan Archives, City of London, ref: MJ/SP/XX/124*)

f. Bill of Indictment, Middlesex Sessions of the Peace, 1651. (*London Metropolitan Archives, City of London, ref: MJ/SP/XX/124*)

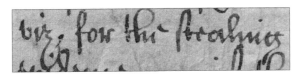

g. Petition, Middlesex Sessions of the Peace, 1670s. (*London Metropolitan Archives, City of London, ref: MJ/SP/XX/198*)

h. Recognizance, Middlesex Sessions of the Peace, 1662. (*London Metropolitan Archives, City of London, ref: MJ/SP/XX/676*)

The new year now begins on 1 January, but until the middle of the eighteenth century in England (and 150 years earlier in Scotland) the year was reckoned from Lady Day, 25 March. In 1752, the 'New Style' was adopted in England, with the year 1752 beginning on 1 January following 31 December 1751. Eleven days were also dropped from the calendar in September of that year, with Thursday, 14 September following Wednesday, 2 September. During the later seventeenth century, a double indication was generally given for the period 1 January–24 March, as shown in Figure 2.4a.

Church festivals were commonly used for dating events in earlier records, but by the seventeenth century, the day and month were given in records either in Latin or English, along with either the regnal year (Figure 2.4b), or the calendar year, or both (Figure 2.4c).

EXERCISE 2.4

For the following transcription and translation exercises, use table 2.II in C.R. Cheney's *A Handbook of Dates* to convert the regnal year to a date. Note that the regnal number comes directly after the name of the monarch, with the regnal year at the end, after the monarch's title ('by the grace of God king of England, Scotland, France and Ireland, defender of the faith etc'). Well into the eighteenth century, records written in English were dated in Latin.

Figure 2.4: Dates in seventeenth-century records.

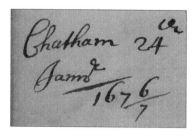

a. Testimonial letter, Navy Board In-Letters. (*The National Archives, ref: ADM 106/322/30*)

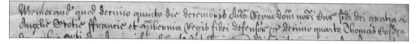

b. Recognizance, Middlesex Sessions of the Peace, 1662. (*London Metropolitan Archives, City of London, ref: MJ/SP/XX/676*)

c. Condition of Bastardy Bond, St Andrew, Enfield, 1704. (*London Metropolitan Archives, City of London, ref: DRO/004/D/06/002. Reproduced by kind permission of the Parish of St Andrew, Enfield*)

EXERCISE 2.5

The following excerpt from 1679 contains characteristic secretary letter forms, including small 'p', 'c' and 'h', and capital 'C', alongside typical italic 'r', 'f' and 's' forms. Note the 'th' ligature used in the second word and elsewhere, though not universally. There are a handful of abbreviations. It is typical of the handwriting found in a wide range of later seventeenth-century records.

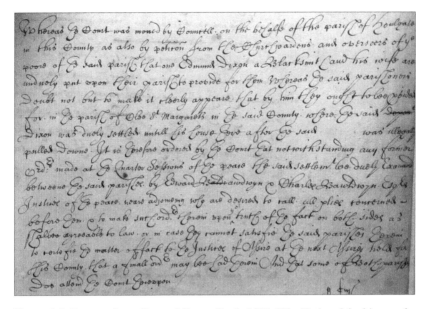

Figure 2.5: Excerpt from Crown Minute Book, 1679. (*The National Archives, ref: ASSI 2/1, p.112*)

EXERCISE 2.6

Before attempting to transcribe and translate the bond in Exercise 2.7 (Figure 2.6c), it will be useful to read through some bonds to gain a familiarity with their structure and language. Look through some of the images of early eighteenth-century typescript bonds in Latin on Ancestry (see, for example, the Norfolk, England, Marriage Bonds 1557–1915 collection), which may be compared with later eighteenth-century bonds in English as an aid to translation from Latin, and also with the bond shown in Figure 2.6c, as an aid to extending any abbreviations that are not used in records written in English.

Final Selections: Excerpts from Late Seventeenth and Early Eighteenth-Century Records

EXERCISE 2.7

The burial register (excerpt a) may look easy to read, but four of the eight entries were mistranscribed in an online index. There are six different marks of abbreviation in the four lines of the late seventeenth-century estreat (excerpt b); note also the accented 'c'.

There are ten different marks of abbreviation in the bond (excerpt c), which you dated in Exercise 2.4. Excerpt d continues the petition shown in Figure 2.3f of the porter 'with noe manner of livelyhood'.

Excerpt e is an example of a typical seventeenth-century court roll entry in Latin, and the very neat mixed handwriting often found in court records of the time; it may be necessary to check some capital letter forms against those in Appendix C, Table C.1. Although there are several typical marks of abbreviation here, the most common is a tiny curl at the end of a terminal letter.

The final two excerpts are examples of the rough hands that will far more commonly be found in late seventeenth-century documents, and which need to be tackled slowly and patiently; it may not be possible to transcribe every word.

Figure 2.6

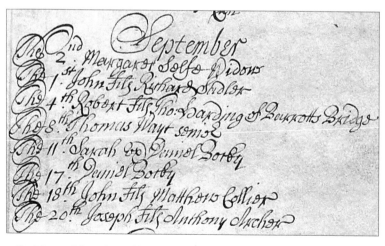

a. Burials, parish register, Cirencester, 1706. (*Gloucestershire Archives, ref: P86/1 IN*)

b. Estreat, Holm Cultram, Cumberland, 1672. (*The National Archives, ref: LR 11/81/924*)

c. Bastardy Bond, St Andrew, Enfield, 1704. (*London Metropolitan Archives, City of London, ref: DRO/004/D/06/002. Reproduced by kind permission of the Parish of St Andrew, Enfield*)

d. Declaration, Middlesex Sessions of the Peace, 1670s. (*London Metropolitan Archives, City of London, ref: MJ/SP/XX/198*)

e. Court Roll, Isleworth, 1683. (*London Metropolitan Archives, City of London, ref: ACC/1379/034. Reproduced by kind permission of the Duke of Northumberland*)

f. Apprenticeship Bond, St Peter Cornhill, 1700. (*London Metropolitan Archives, City of London, ref: P69/PET1/B/033/MS04200. Reproduced by kind permission of the Parish of St Helen, Bishopsgate*)

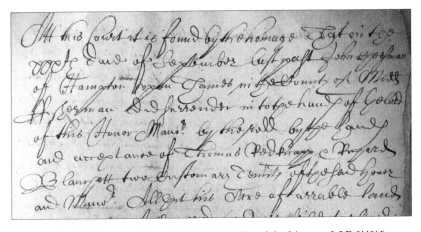

g. Court book, Hampton Court, 1659. (*The National Archives, ref: LR 3/40/4*)

Further Practice and Resources for Reading Later Seventeenth-Century Hands

It is always useful to compare your own attempts at transcription with model answers: there are four plates of later seventeenth and early eighteenth-century Essex parish records with transcriptions and notes in Hilda Grieve's *Examples of English Handwriting 1150–1750*; there are also several plates with transcriptions and commentaries in Hilary Marshall's *Palaeography for Family and Local Historians*. A variety of documents from the sixteenth and seventeenth centuries from a range of archives are provided in Mark Forrest's *Reading Early Handwriting 1500–1700*.

For further practice reading lists of names, read through and transcribe some late seventeenth-century City of London records in Ancestry's London, England, Land Tax Records 1692–1932 collection. For practice reading a variety of different hands, with some challenging grammar and spellings, there are hundreds of late seventeenth-century inventories in Ancestry's Gloucestershire, England, Wills and Inventories, 1541–1858 collection. For some preliminary practice reading Latin, first look through some of the post-1733 probate clauses written in English, which are found at the end of wills, and then transcribe and translate some of the early eighteenth-century probate clauses that were written in Latin.

3. The Sixteenth Century: Records in English

- Elizabethan secretary hand
- Letters taking more than one form
- Numbers and money
- Dates in sixteenth-century records

This chapter examines records written in English from around the middle of the sixteenth century to the early seventeenth century. Elizabethan records, such as wills, inventories, accounts, letters, parish registers, deeds and evidence in court cases, are potentially of huge interest to genealogists and historians, but are inaccessible without some familiarity with the secretary hand.

We have already seen the persistence of some secretary letter forms – 'c', 'r', 's' and particularly 'e' – well into the eighteenth century. Here, we look at Elizabethan secretary hands, which may employ a number of different forms of individual letters, often within the same word, and are often characterised by broken strokes, 'horns' on the tops of letters, long approach strokes, and small rounded loops on ascenders.

Figure 3.1 shows the small letter forms that are particularly characteristic of Elizabethan scripts:

a	_a_	_n_	_a_
c	_c_	_r_	
e	_e_	_e_	
g	_g_		
h	_h_	_c_	
p	_p_	_p_	
r	_r_	_e_	_z_
s	_s_	_r_	
w	_w_		
x	_x_		
y	_y_		

Figure 3.1: Characteristic Elizabethan secretary letters.

EXERCISE 3.1

Before attempting to read continuous prose in a later sixteenth-century hand, refer to Appendix A.2, which covers some of the terms used to describe elements of script and to describe different letter forms, then transcribe the following words, which are all taken from the letter in Exercise 3.2.

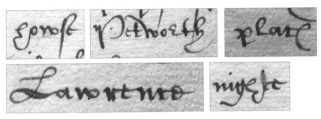

Figure 3.2: Examples of characteristic secretary letters. (*Letter in the Loseley MSS papers of Sir Christopher and Sir William More, Surrey History Centre, ref: 6729/7/83. Reproduced by kind permission of the More-Molyneux family and Surrey History Centre*)

EXERCISE 3.2

Transcribe the following letter, which is written in a very clear late sixteenth-century secretary hand. There are a few marks of abbreviation, and a punctuation mark:

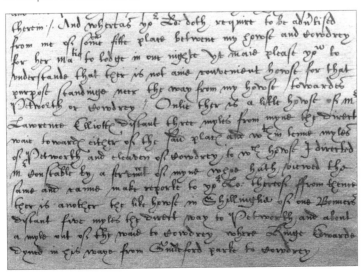

Figure 3.3: Letter, 1591. (*Letter in the Loseley MSS papers of Sir Christopher and Sir William More, Surrey History Centre, ref: 6729/7/83. Reproduced by kind permission of the More-Molyneux family and Surrey History Centre*)

There are thousands of digitised images of the copy wills that make up the National Archives series PROB11, available to browse on Ancestry, in the England and Wales, Prerogative Court of Canterbury Wills, 1384–1858, collection. The wills were copied by clerks into the registers in a neat, uniform hand, making them ideal sixteenth-century reading practice.

Transcribe two or three wills from any of the later sixteenth-century pieces, checking capital letters against typical letters in Appendix C.1. All the abbreviations that will be found have already been covered, apart from the 'sir'/ 'ser' abbreviation, one form of which is shown in Appendix D.1, and the very common practice of running the definite article into the following word when it starts with a vowel. See Figure 3.4a, 'I first betake my soule into thands [the hands] of thallmightie [the almighty]', and Figure 3.4b 'my maide servante Isabell Plumleye'.

Figure 3.4: Common sixteenth-century abbreviations.

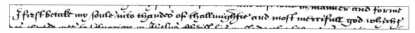

a. (*The National Archives, ref: PROB 11/64/38*)

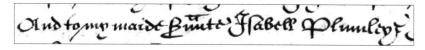

b. Copy will, 1581. (*The National Archives, ref: PROB 11/64/38*)

Many Elizabethan records, however, were not written by professional scribes. Refer to the Elizabethan secretary forms in Appendix C.1 for help transcribing the following excerpts from original wills, written either by the testator or a local clerk.

EXERCISE 3.3

Transcribe the following excerpts from sixteenth-century original wills. Wills may run to a few lines or several pages, but they all tend to follow the same form, generally beginning 'In the name of God, Amen', followed by the date, name of the testator and a note that he or she is sound of mind though sick of body:

Figure 3.5: Excerpts from sixteenth-century original wills.

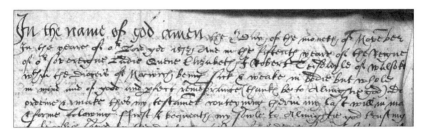

a. Will of Robert Teisdayle, 1573. (*The National Archives, ref: PROB 10/79*)

Before making bequests, the soul is offered to God, and the body given for burial:

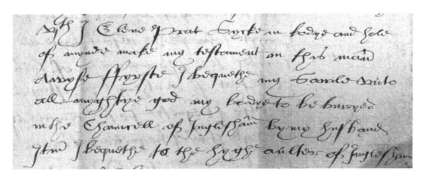

b. Will of Elene Prat, 1547. (*The National Archives, ref: PROB 10/33*)

A list of bequests follows, often starting with a contribution to the poor of the parish:

c. Will of Elyner Baker, 1563. (*The National Archives, ref: PROB 10/53*)

The remainder of the goods after debts and expenses are bequeathed and the executor or executrix of the will is named:

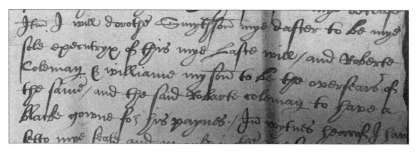

d. Will of Thomas Smytheson, 1563. (*The National Archives, ref: PROB 10/53*)

The probate clause is written at the end of the will in a formulaic and – as here – highly abbreviated Latin; the only point of interest is that it gives the date by which the testator must have died:

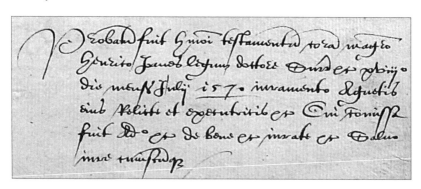

e. Will of John Altam, St George, Southwark, probate year 1570.
(*London Metropolitan Archives, City of London, ref: DW/PA/05/1570/023. Reproduced by kind permission of the Diocese of Winchester*)

Many sixteenth-century wills were written clearly and are easy to read with a little practice. Those that were written hurriedly in an uneducated hand may often be deciphered without too much difficulty because they follow the typical will template.

EXERCISE 3.4

Transcribe the following excerpts from sixteenth-century parish registers, which cover most of the different letter forms that are likely to be encountered in records from the period. Many parish registers are available to view online; after this exercise, transcribe sections of sixteenth-century parish registers, and correct the online indexes where necessary.

Figure 3.6: Excerpts from parish registers.

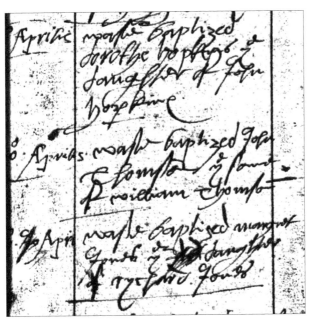

a. Baptism Register, All Saints, Kingston upon Thames, 1575. (*Surrey History Centre, ref: P33/1/3*)

b. Baptism Register, Salisbury St Edmund, 1595–96. (*Wiltshire and Swindon Heritage Centre, ref: 1901/1. Accessed on Ancestry.co.uk*)

c. Burial Register, Salisbury St Edmund, 1592. (*Wiltshire and Swindon Heritage Centre, ref: 1901/1. Accessed on Ancestry.co.uk*)

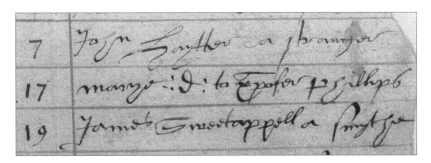

d. Burial Register, Salisbury St Edmund, 1595. (*Wiltshire and Swindon Heritage Centre, ref: 1901/1. Accessed on Ancestry.co.uk*)

e. Marriage Register, St James, Clerkenwell, 1610. (*London Metropolitan Archives, City of London, ref: P76/JS1/004. Reproduced by kind permission of the Parish of St James, Clerkenwell*)

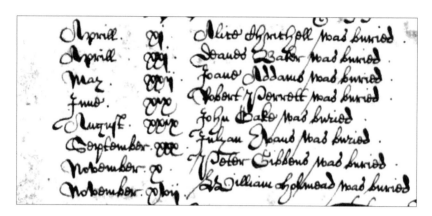

f. Burial Register, Abbotsbury, Dorset, 1589. (*Dorset History Centre, ref: PE/ABB RE 1/1*)

Note the following example of the middle-English 'yogh' character (Figure 3.7), which was used in the vernacular into the sixteenth century to represent the sounds 'y', 'g' or 'z', but was far more commonly used earlier ('& pays yerly'):

Figure 3.7: An example of the yogh in the Rental of Freeholders, Rothwell, Yorkshire, 1528. (*The National Archives, ref: SC 11/757*)

EXERCISE 3.5

Transcribe the excerpts in Figure 3.8, which come from a selection of sixteenth-century inventories and accounts. Most unfamiliar words in the following excerpts will be found in Stuart Raymond's *Words From Wills and Other Probate Records*, Joy Bristow's *The Local Historian's Glossary of Words and Terms*, and Rosemary Milward's *A Glossary of Household, Farming and Trade Terms from Probate Inventories*.

This list of goods is written in a very clear Elizabethan secretary hand. For a definition of the word in the eighth line, try an online search, or J.O. Halliwell, *A Handbook of Archaic and Provincial Words*:

Figure 3.8: Excerpts from sixteenth-century lists and accounts.

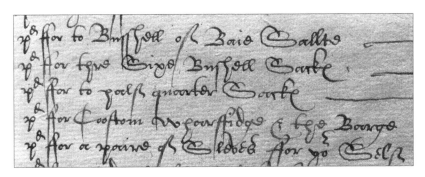

a. Schedule of Goods, Bills in the Mayor's Court, City of London, 1587–88. (*London Metropolitan Archives, City of London, ref: CLA/024/02/017*)

Note here the small letter 'a' with a horizontal line over the top, making it easy to mistake for 'oi', which is particularly clear in the word 'half' in line 3:

b. Servant's Account, Loseley MSS Papers of Sir Christopher and Sir William More, 1589. (*Surrey History Centre, ref: 6729/7/82. Reproduced by kind permission of the More-Molyneux family and Surrey History Centre*)

Before attempting excerpt c, part of a mid-sixteenth-century probate inventory, examine the following words, which show the z-form 'r', the 'u' and 'v' forms of 'u', and an extreme form of the non-bodied 'h'. The upstroke at the end of the letter 'n', which appears throughout the document, does not appear to indicate an abbreviation:

'hire beste Frocke' (her best frock)

'on troffe on tunne' (one trough one tun)

'forcke and tubes' (fork and tubs)

The following, from the same source, is the most challenging excerpt so far:

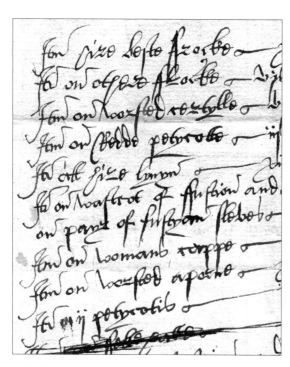

c. **Probate Inventory of Robert Blackmore,** *c*.1550. (*Essex Record Office, ref: D/ ABW 3/172*)

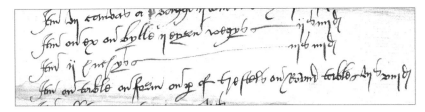

d. **Probate Inventory of Robert Blackmore, *c*.1550. (*Essex Record Office, ref: D/ABW 3/172*)**

EXERCISE 3.6

This exercise introduces some more difficult writing from mid- to late-sixteenth-century letters.

The salutation and leave-taking here is commonly found in letters of this period, and the spurred 'a' and x-form 'p' are characteristic of this date:

Figure 3.9: Excerpts from sixteenth-century letters.

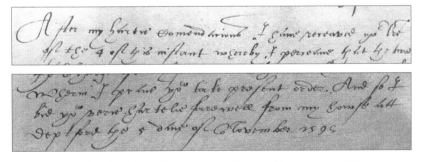

a. **Letter from Charles, Lord Howard, to the Deputy Lieutenants of Surrey, 5 November 1595. (*Surrey History Centre, ref: 6729/13/82. Reproduced by kind permission of the More-Molyneux family and Surrey History Centre*)**

Here, a whole letter gives continuous reading practice. There is a long descender on the final letter 'n', making it look like a modern cursive 'y' (as in 'wryten' at the end of line 1), and the final letter 'u' is similar to this (as in 'you' at the end of line 3). The letter 'c' is more curved in shape than any example seen so far, and wherever the definite article is followed by a word beginning with a vowel, it runs into that word.

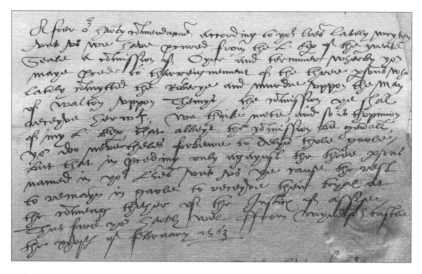

b. Letter from Privy Council to Sir Henry Weston, William Moore and Richard Bydon, 26 February 1595. (*Surrey History Centre, ref: 6729/10/24. Reproduced by kind permission of the More-Molyneux family and Surrey History Centre*)

Examine the following words before attempting the final two excerpts from a sixteenth-century letter:

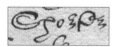 'Shorter': a distinct z-form 'r':

 'chasse': again, a curved right-angled 'c':

 'borders': an unusual but by no means uncommon form of the letter 'b', and an open 'd', make several words in this letter difficult to decipher:

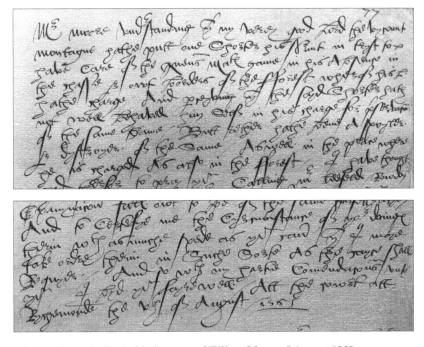

c. Letter from the Earl of Leicester to William Moore, 5 August 1565.
(*Surrey History Centre, ref: 6729/3/13. Reproduced by kind permission of the*
More-Molyneux family and Surrey History Centre)

Numbers and Money

Arabic numerals were often used in dates from the early sixteenth century as
well as, or in place of, Roman numerals or dating by regnal year. Numerals
may not be instantly recognisable.

Figure 3.10: Examples of Arabic numerals in sixteenth-century records.

'xxvii[th] of September 1574':

a. Letter from Thomas Browne to William More. (*Surrey History Centre, ref: LM*
COR/3/167. Reproduced by kind permission of the More-Molyneux family and
Surrey History Centre)

'... Anno D[omi]ni 1542':

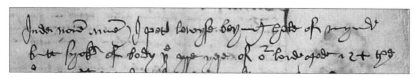

b. Will of Katherine Masson, Saint Olave, Southwark, probate year 1544. (*London Metropolitan Archives, City of London, ref: DW/PA/05/1544/010. Reproduced by kind permission of the Diocese of Winchester*)

'... I pet[er] lewyse beying hole of mynde butt syck of body the yere of o[u]r lord god 154 [ie: 1540] ...':

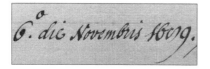

c. Will of Peter Lewyse, Diocese of London, probate year 1540. (*London Metropolitan Archives, City of London, ref: DL/AL/C/003/MS09052/001A, Will 55. Reproduced by kind permission of the Diocese of London*)

'6° die Novembris 1689':

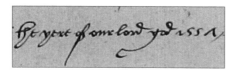

d. Inventory, City of London. (*London Metropolitan Archives, City of London, ref: CLA/040/02/007*)

'the yere of our lord god 1557':

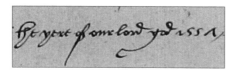

e. Will of William Adlington, Southwark, probate year 1557. (*London Metropolitan Archives, City of London, ref: DW/PA/05/1557/055. Reproduced by kind permission of the Diocese of Winchester*)

'The last wyll and testament of me John Motley made the 29 of August 1557':

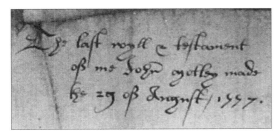

f. Will of John Motley, probate year 1557. (*London Metropolitan Archives, City of London, ref: DW/PA/05/1557/12/01. Reproduced by kind permission of the Diocese of Winchester*)

'An[n]o d[omi]ni 1574':

g. Parish Register, Brookthorpe, Gloucestershire. (*Gloucestershire Archives, ref: GDR/VI/47*)

See Appendix E, Numbers, for other 'difficult' Arabic numerals.

Roman numerals were used interchangeably with words and, as they were often joined together, may perhaps be mistaken for words. Superscript letters following Roman numerals indicate ordinal numbers, in the same way that they are used today as, for example, in '10th' for 'tenth'. (In the second example (b) in Figure 3.10 above, the superscript ° signifies that the numeral 6 represents the Latin ablative ordinal 'sexto' – 'on the sixth day of November 1689'). Superscript letters may also be found following numbers used from habit, where they have no real meaning at all. A superscript number following a Roman numeral indicates a multiplier.

Figure 3.11: Examples of Roman numerals in sixteenth-century records.

'It[e]m i plate Candlesticke, one litle brasse pott iij litle pott[es] – viij d':

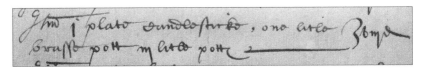

a. Schedule of Goods, Mayor's Court, City of London, 1587. (*London Metropolitan Archives, City of London, ref: CLA/024/02/019*)

'ix[th] of September 1572':

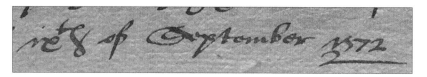

b. Letter. (*Surrey History Centre, ref: 6729/10/38. Reproduced by kind permission of the More-Molyneux family and Surrey History Centre*)

'It[e]m iiij[or] table clothes ii[o] towell[es]': the superscript letters probably refer to the Latin words 'quattuor' and 'duo' for 'four' and 'two', although the document was written in English:

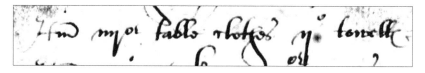

c. Thomas Smith Inventory, Berkeley, 1587. (*Gloucestershire Archives, ref: 270138, Inventory 12*)

'It[e]m xxiiij[ty] yardes of painted clothes – viij s': xxiiij should be read as 'four and twenty':

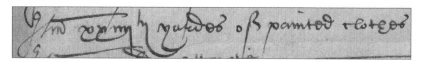

d. Schedule of goods, Mayor's Court, City of London, 1587. (*London Metropolitan Archives, City of London, ref: CLA/024/02/019*)

'In the name of god amen the xviith Daie of Octob[e]r in the yere of o[u]r lord v[c] xlv' – the superscript [c] is a multiplier, so the date is 545, i.e. 1545):

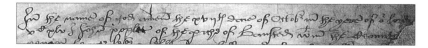

e. Will of John Poplet, Banstead, Surrey, probate year 1545. (*London Metropolitan Archives, City of London, ref: DW/PA/05/1545/013. Reproduced by kind permission of the Diocese of Winchester*)

EXERCISE 3.7

Referring to Appendix E, if necessary, transcribe the following as written, then put the dates into their modern form:

Figure 3.12: Dates in sixteenth-century records.

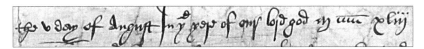

a. Will of Robert Bedyll, Compton, Surrey. (*London Metropolitan Archives, City of London, ref: DW/PA/05/1543/003. Reproduced by kind permission of the Diocese of Winchester*)

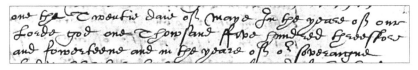

b. Will of John Kingstone, Surbiton, Surrey. (*London Metropolitan Archives, City of London, ref: DW/PA/05/1574/034. Reproduced by kind permission of the Diocese of Winchester*)

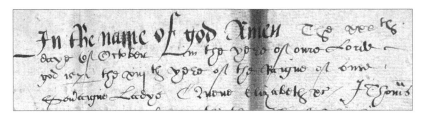

c. Will of Thomas Kynne, Minchinhampton, Gloucestershire. (*The National Archives, ref: PROB 10/79*)

Roman numerals were used for accounting purposes, with the currency denominations of pounds, shillings and pence denoted by superscript letters (see Appendix E, Money). 'This Som Comethe to xxi^{li} ix^s x$^{d'}$ is transcribed as £21 9s 10d:

Figure 3.13: Money in sixteenth-century records. (*Servants' Account; Surrey History Centre, ref: 6729/7/82. Reproduced by kind permission of the More-Molyneux family and Surrey History Centre*)

Final Selections: Excerpts from Sixteenth and Early Seventeenth-Century Records in English

EXERCISE 3.8

Money features in excerpt b of the final selection of excerpts from sixteenth and early seventeenth-century records in English. Excerpt e is from a court roll written in Latin; difficult words and phrases are helpfully written in English. A wide range of abbreviations and different letter forms are used throughout.

Figure 3.14: Excerpts from sixteenth and early seventeenth-century records in English.

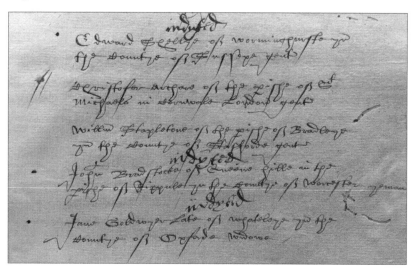

a. List of prisoners in the Clink prison for religion, 23 July 1582, Loseley MSS. (*Surrey History Centre, ref: 6729/10/53. Reproduced by kind permission of the More-Molyneux family and Surrey History Centre*)

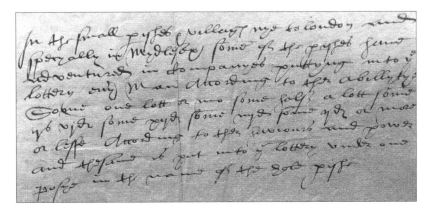

b. Lord Mayor Adventurers in Lottery, no date, Loseley MSS. (*Surrey History Centre, ref: 6729/7/144. Reproduced by kind permission of the More-Molyneux family and Surrey History Centre*)

c. Rental, Hull, Yorkshire, 1649. (*The National Archives, ref: SC 11/749*)

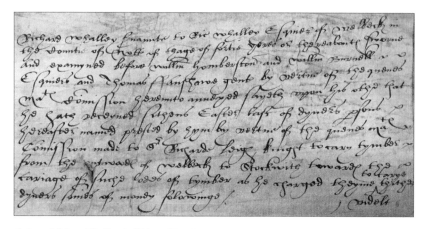

d. Inquisition, Welbeck Abbey, Nottinghamshire, 1566. (*The National Archives, ref: E 178/3062*)

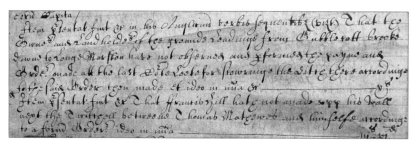

e. Court roll, Crown Manor of Tring, 1648–49. (*The National Archives, ref: LR 3/30/3*)

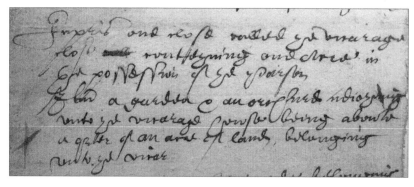

f. Terrier, East Betchworth, Surrey, 1614. (*London Metropolitan Archives, City of London, ref: DW/S/009/A. Reproduced by kind permission of the Diocese of Winchester*)

g. Copy Will of John Dyer of Frating, Essex, May 1573. (*The National Archives, ref: PROB 11/55/267*)

Further Practice and Resources for Reading Elizabethan Hands

Most county record offices have excellent parish register transcripts, published by local societies early in the twentieth century, available on open access shelves, which may be used for checking your own attempts at transcribing sixteenth-century records. Then look at one of the mid-sixteenth-century registers available online, such as St John at Hackney (in Ancestry's London, England, Church of England Baptisms, Marriages and Burials, 1538–1812 collection), transcribe them and submit corrections for some of the mistakes in the online indexes.

When reading sixteenth-century inventories, the three glossaries referred to in Exercise 3.5, along with *The Shorter Oxford English Dictionary* and J.O. Halliwell's *A Handbook of Archaic and Provincial Words* will cover most of the unfamiliar words encountered. Before starting out, read through a volume of probate inventories published by one of the many county record societies, such as *Surrey Probate Inventories 1558–1603* (Surrey Record Society, Volume xxxix) to gain a thorough familiarity with the names of garments, cloths, household and agricultural implements, and also with the idiosyncrasies of sixteenth-century spelling (such as the common practice of starting a word beginning with a vowel following the indefinite article with an 'n'; for example, 'an inventory' written as 'a ninventory').

Many of the published volumes of probate inventories also contain useful glossaries of dialect and doubtful words. F.W. Steer's volume of *Farm and Cottage Inventories of Mid-Essex 1635–1749* contains a hugely useful general introduction to homes and furnishings, eating and drinking, and household and village industries.

For standard Elizabethan secretary reading practice, there is a Privy Council letter from 1576 with a transcript, and further follow-up letters, on the University of Cambridge's Faculty of English 'English Handwriting 1500–1700' online course.

For practice transcribing a variety of records, there are several books and pamphlets containing plates of sixteenth-century documents with accompanying transcriptions. See, for example, Hilda Grieve's *Examples of English Handwriting 1150–1750*, Hilary Marshall's *Palaeography for Family and Local Historians*, L.C. Hector's *The Handwriting of English Documents* and Mark Forrest's *Reading Early Handwriting 1500–1700*.

There is useful commentary on the secretary alphabet, along with a few facsimiles and transcriptions of documents, in Lionel Munby's *Reading Tudor and Stuart Handwriting. Elizabethan Handwriting 1500–1650* by G.E. Dawson and L. Kennedy-Skipton contains several facsimiles of examples of textbook secretary hands, along with some examples of documents written in idiosyncratic and hasty hands.

There are excerpts from a range of documents, including parish registers, parish accounts, court rolls and vestry minutes, along with an excellent example of a 'pure' secretary hand, in F.G. Emmison, *How to Read Local Archives 1550–1700*. There are also facsimiles of a wide range of records including wills, probate inventories, letters and evidences in ecclesiastical court cases, all with accompanying transcriptions, in P.M. Hoskin, S.L. Slinn and C.C. Webb, *Reading the Past: Sixteenth and Seventeenth Century English Handwriting*, one of the Borthwick Palaeography Guides available from the Borthwick Institute for Archives at the University of York.

For an example of the research that may be undertaken using wills and sessions rolls, see F.G. Emmison, *Elizabeth Life*, which looks at a wide range of topics, from furniture and furnishings to employment, offences and trade.

4. The Sixteenth Century: Records in Latin

- Record type
- Abbreviations in Latin
- Dates in sixteenth-century records in Latin
- Sixteenth and early seventeenth-century manor court records

This chapter examines the handwriting of late sixteenth and seventeenth-century records such as parish registers and manor court rolls, which were written in Latin, are of significant interest to genealogists and local historians, and may be understood with a minimal understanding of the Latin language.

All of the letter forms have already been covered, but Latin was abbreviated to a far greater extent than English, and a good understanding of the system of marks and symbols used is necessary when attempting to read these documents. All the general and special marks of abbreviation are shown in Appendix D.2, but a useful, practical way of gaining familiarity with the elaborate system of abbreviation in Latin is to transcribe a few pages of those sources that were published in 'record type' in the nineteenth and early twentieth centuries.

Record type was a special typeface used by the Record Commissioners for the printing of the early nineteenth-century folio series, with the aim of reproducing in print the abbreviation marks and special symbols used in the writing of medieval and early modern manuscripts. Stylised forms of abbreviation marks were reproduced, and each mark was intended to be extended by the reader, according to rule. Figure 4.1 shows some general rules for extending the marks used in record type; for more unusual meanings, refer to Appendix D.2.

The most common mark used is the general mark of abbreviation, a wavy line over or through the ascender of a letter or letters, which, according to rule, should indicate the omission of one or more letters, either before or after the letter marked, or both, but was often used as a general mark of abbreviation, particularly in the publications of local record societies. Unlike the special marks, this mark does not indicate which particular letters are missing. For this reason, Charles Trice Martin's *The Record Interpreter*, which lists abbreviated words by contracted form rather than extended form, is invaluable.

For all the following exercises, have *The Record Interpreter*, the select word list from Eileen Gooder's *Latin for Local History*, and a classical Latin dictionary to hand; always refer to Gooder's select word list and table of commonly abbreviated words and phrases before turning to other reference works.

Figure 4.1: General rules for extending marks and symbols used in record type

festū   straight line over a letter: supply 'm' or 'n' following the marked letter ('festum')

Iõ ip̃e   wavy line over letter or through ascender: supply one or more letters before or after the marked letter ('ideo ipse')

in miᵃ·   superior letter: supply a letter or letters, one of which is the superior letter itself ('misericordia')

For these special marks, supply the following letters in place of the marks:

v3 omnib3   'et' or 'us' ('videlicet', 'omnibus')

p̃   'er' or 're' ('pre')

min⁹   (above line of writing) 'us' or 'os' ('minus'); (even with line of writing) 'com' or 'con'

campoȝ   'rum' or 'run' ('camporum')

Wellₑ   'es' or 'is' ('Welles')

For these symbols, supply the following words:

⁊   'et'

⁊c : &c.   'et cetera'

For the following letter modifications, read:

p̃x̃   'pro' ('proximo')

p   'pre'

EXERCISE 4.1

Following the rules for extending marks, transcribe and extend all the abbreviations in the excerpts in Figure 4.2, then translate into English. For excerpt b, refer to Appendix E on dates if necessary, and also convert the date to modern form.

Figure 4.2: Excerpts from court rolls published in record type.

Et q̃d Thomᵃs Wattᵱ unus tenenciũ d̃ni, de novo crexit duas cruces in coĩa de Wymbildon, p quod tenenĩ Abb̃is Westñĩ ꝉ tenenĩ alioᴈ d̃ñoᴈ, in Wannys-worth, clamant injuste hẽr coĩam infᵃˑ limites antiquas coĩs hujᵒ d̃nii; in p̃judiciũ d̃ni ꝉ teneñ : Iõ prec̃ est bedelꝉ, q̃d scĩr fac̃ eiđm Thome, q̃d sit ad px̃ cur̃, ad respond̃ d̃no, de p̃miss ꝉ q̃d insup remover̃ fac̃ cruc̃ p̃dic̃, sub peᵃˑ for̃ teñ ꝉ terr̃ suoᴈ, que tenet de d̃no, scđm consuetuđ man̄ij ꝉc.

a. View of Frankpledge, Putney, 5 June 1492. (*Extracts from the Court Rolls of the Manor of Wimbledon, Wimbledon Common Committee, 1866*)

Wymbildon.—Curia Generaꝉ ejusđm loci, tenĩ apud Putneth, die Lune px̃ ante festũ ap̃ploᴈ Simonis ꝉ Jude, 1 Hen. VII.

*   *   *   *   *   *

(m. 1.)

Homagiũ.—Compĩ est p inquĩs homagij vᴣ p sacr̃m Thome Pentecost [et septem aꝉ]   * * *

Et p̃senĩ q̃d Joñesᵛⁱⁱʲᵈ Bonar, vend̃ bosc̃ extᵃnijs, in coĩa de Wymbildoñ, contᵃ cons̃ ; ĩo in ñia.   Et q̃d Ric̃usᵛʲᵈ Bonhᵃm occup̃ coĩam de Wymbildon, ubi nulꝉ coĩam haberet : Iõ ip̃e in miᵃˑ

Miᵃ ijs iiijᵈ

b. Court Roll, Wimbledon. (*Extracts from the Court Rolls of the Manor of Wimbledon, Wimbledon Common Committee, 1866*)

A considerable number of historical records were printed by the Record Commission, and many local record societies also printed series such as sessions rolls or court rolls in record type in the nineteenth and early twentieth centuries. Many of these are cheaply available online and provide excellent practice for reading records written in Latin.

EXERCISE 4.2

Transcribe and translate the following excerpts from Elizabethan parish registers. Registers written in Latin are generally only lightly abbreviated, although the handwriting may be challenging. Large numbers of registers are available to view online for further practice.

In the first excerpt, the sign 𝓞 is used even with the line of writing to signify the letters 'us'; the other abbreviations have already been met in writings in English, and the handwriting is typical of Elizabethan parish registers.

Lists of names often pose significant difficulties for volunteer indexers, and many online indexes of sixteenth-century records are not as useful as they should be because of mistranscriptions of unfamiliar capital letters and abbreviated Latin forenames.

EXERCISE 4.3

Transcribe the following list of names. In the translation, change the Latin names to their English equivalents, as should always be done when indexing; there is a useful list of Latin forenames in *The Record Interpreter*. Retain the spellings of surnames, which will never be found in Latin form at this date. 'Gen' is the abbreviation form of 'generosus' (gentleman), and all the men were sworn as jurors ('juratores').

Figure 4.3: Excerpts from sixteenth-century parish registers written in Latin.

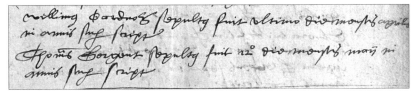

a. Parish Register, English Bicknor, Gloucestershire, 1587. (*Gloucestershire Archives, ref: GDR/VI/34*)

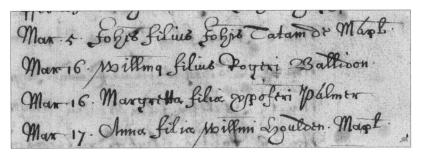

b. Parish Register, Ashbourne St Oswald, Derbyshire, 1578. (*Derbyshire Record Office, ref: D662/A/PI/1/1*)

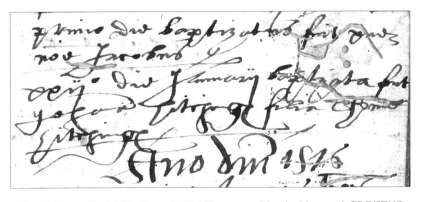

c. Brookthorpe Parish Register, 1576. (*Gloucestershire Archives, ref: GDR/VI/47*)

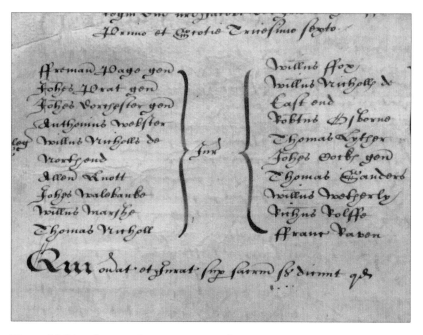

Figure 4.4: List of names from a seventeenth-century court roll. View of Frankpledge, Court Baron, Haringay and Hornsey, 11 May 1603. (*The National Archives, ref: SC 2/191/8*)

Manor court records provide a rich and often continuous source of information about named individuals and places from the end of the thirteenth century to the end of the sixteenth century, when many manorial responsibilities were transferred to the parish churchwardens and vestry. A range of matters were covered in the manorial courts, such as the payment of dues and services, the regulation of disputes concerning personal matters such as debt and trespass, the maintenance of law and order at the local level, and the control and registration of tenancies, all of potential interest to genealogists.

EXERCISE 4.4

The following two short excerpts from manor court records demonstrate a range of abbreviations and abbreviated phrases and introduce some typical court business. Transcribe and translate into English.

Figure 4.5: Excerpts from seventeenth-century court rolls.

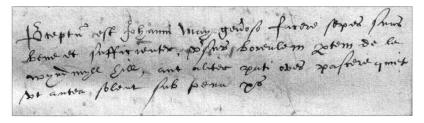

a. Court Book, Manor Court of West Stoke, 1604. (*The National Archives, ref: WARD 2/26/94/14*)

b. Court Roll of Manor Court of Finchley, 24 April 1621. (*The National Archives, ref: SC 2/191/7*)

EXERCISE 4.5

The following longer excerpt provides some continuous reading practice. All of the typical marks of abbreviation are used, but in many cases the mark of abbreviation is little more than a small mark at the end of a word. It may help, when transcribing the first line, to know that this is a page from a court book of the manor of Isleworth.

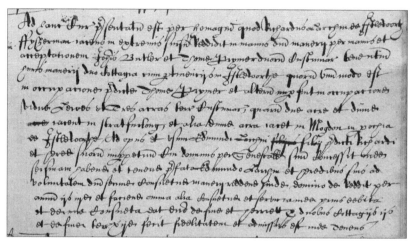

Figure 4.6: Excerpt from the seventeenth-century court book for the Manor of Isleworth, 22 October 1612. (*London Metropolitan Archives, City of London, ref: ACC/1379/026. Reproduced by kind permission of the Duke of Northumberland*)

It should be clear from Figure 4.3c that sixteenth- and seventeenth-century documents written in Latin may be difficult to decipher, not only because of the unfamiliar letter forms and language, but also because they were simply badly written. This is especially true of parish registers, which were often written in an uneducated hand, and draft documents that were intended to be enrolled at a later date.

EXERCISE 4.6

Transcribe and translate the following excerpt from the proceedings of a court of survey for Stratford manor in Suffolk. This was a draft document, hurriedly written and highly abbreviated. It may not be possible to be sure of every word, but useful information, such as personal names and the names and locations of plots of land, may certainly be extracted.

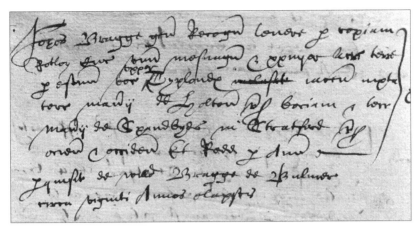

Figure 4.7: Excerpt from the seventeenth-century draft court book for the Manor of Stratford, Suffolk, 1619–20. (*The National Archives, ref: DL 44/1040. Duchy copyright material in the National Archives is the property of Her Majesty the Queen in Right of Her Duchy of Lancaster. This image is reproduced by permission of the Chancellor and the Council of the Duchy of Lancaster*)

Final Selections: Excerpts from Sixteenth and Seventeenth-Century Records in Latin

EXERCISE 4.7

The final selection of records for transcription includes (excerpt a) a coroner's inquisition concerning a death in Newgate Gaol at the end of the sixteenth century – a remarkable number of prisoners died from 'divine visitation' – and (excerpt b) an early seventeenth-century manor court book. Excerpt c continues the draft court book of Exercise 4.6.

The final excerpt, from another coroner's inquisition from 1590, provides extended reading practice in an Elizabethan engrossing secretary hand, which is exceptionally clear, and demonstrates how much interesting detail – often conveniently rendered into English – may be found in these records. A wide range of abbreviations used in Latin will be found here.

Figure 4.8: Excerpts from sixteenth and seventeenth-century documents written in Latin.

a. Coroner's Inquisition on John Smith, 20 May 1590. (*London Metropolitan Archives, City of London, ref: CLA/041/IQ/01/011*)

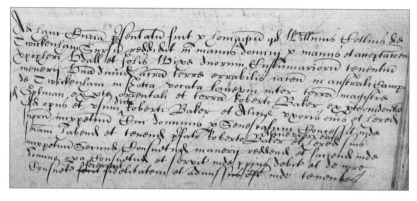

b. Court Book, Isleworth Manor, 1608. (*London Metropolitan Archives, City of London, ref: ACC/1379/026. Reproduced by kind permission of the Duke of Northumberland*)

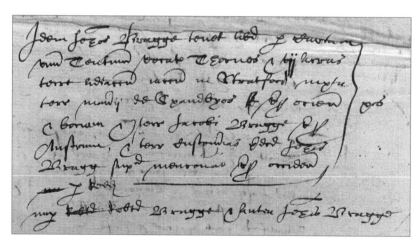

c. Draft Court Book, Manor of Stratford, Suffolk, 1619–20. (*The National Archives, ref: DL 44/1040. Duchy copyright material in the National Archives is the property of Her Majesty the Queen in Right of Her Duchy of Lancaster. This image is reproduced by permission of the Chancellor and the Council of the Duchy of Lancaster*)

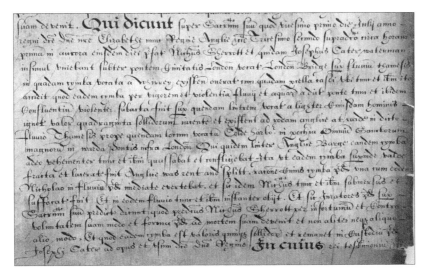

d. Coroner's Inquisition on Nicholas Sherrott, 23 July 1590. (*London Metropolitan Archives, City of London, ref: CLA/041/IQ/01/011*)

Further Practice and Resources for Reading Sixteenth and Seventeenth-Century Records in Latin

There are several reference works that are essential when attempting to read documents written in Latin. Eileen Gooder's *Latin for Local History* has a select word list that covers anything likely to be encountered in parish registers or simple court roll entries. The book is also a useful guide for anyone who wishes to learn to read Latin from scratch.

Charles Trice Martin's *The Record Interpreter* lists every abbreviation likely to be found and contains a useful glossary and a list of Latin place names and Christian names. There is an exhaustive word list in the monumental *Dictionary of Medieval Latin from British Sources*, which is available online from two platforms under licence from the British Academy, but the extensive word list in the *Revised Medieval Latin Word-List* by R.E. Latham will be sufficient for the words found in sixteenth and seventeenth-century records. As none of these reference works also list words found in classical Latin, a dictionary such as the *Oxford Latin Desk Dictionary* is also necessary.

The English Manor c.1200–c.1500 by Mark Bailey is a general introduction to both the structure and composition of the English manor and the principal manorial records, and contains translations of key documents. It also has a glossary and a guide to secondary works that should be consulted before researching court records. For a structured and comprehensive guide to using manorial records, with several exercises in the transcription and translation of a range of records, see *Manorial Records* by Denis Stuart; together these books make an excellent starting point for beginning research on manor court rolls.

There are facsimiles of several manorial documents, with transcriptions and translations and notes on abbreviations in Hilda Grieve's *Examples of English Handwriting 1150–1750*, and plates of sixteenth and seventeenth-century manuscripts with transcriptions and translations in *Widworthy Manorial Court Rolls 1453–1617*, edited by Edwin Haydon and John Harrop.

Many record societies have published selections from local courts rolls and are useful for gaining a familiarity with the Latin vocabulary and the business of the courts. The Selden Society's *Select Cases in Manorial Courts 1250–1550*, edited by L.P. Poos and Lloyd Bonfield, contains a large selection of cases in Latin with expert English translations, as well as a very helpful introduction to the customs and law in the manor courts of different areas. The Oxford Record Society's *Manorial Records of Cuxham, Oxfordshire*, edited by P.D.A. Harvey, contains transcriptions of charters, terriers, account and court records, and tax assessments, and has a glossary of words and spellings not included in classical dictionaries or Latham's *Medieval Latin Word-List*.

Parallel English/Latin texts are particularly useful when learning to read documents in Latin. See, for example, the London County Council's *Court Rolls of Tooting Beck Manor*, and the London Borough of Sutton's *Courts of the Manors of Bandon and Beddington 1498–1552*.

5. Court Hands

- Fifteenth-century secretary and anglicana letter forms
- Legal records
- Chancery and Exchequer records

This chapter examines the handwriting of records written in distinctive 'set' hands up until the early eighteenth century in the various courts of law and government departments, and the handwriting of medieval records in general. There were two main documentary hands in use in medieval times. The first were the Gothic cursives used from the thirteenth century, known as 'court hands', which were well developed and established in England by the mid-fourteenth century and were given the name 'anglicana' in the discipline of manuscript studies in the mid-twentieth century because of their distinctive English character. The second was a version of secretary, which was imported from France and was in general use in England by the end of the fourteenth century.

There are good reasons for gaining familiarity with these scripts. A huge number of records were written in court hands and contain dated references to individuals that may be of interest to genealogists. These range, for example, from early eighteenth-century manor court books containing information on named individuals and land holdings, to fourteenth-century records of the ecclesiastical courts concerning moral offences.

Legal records of all sorts contain information on named individuals for a period of well over 200 years before parish registers begin. Furthermore, just as Elizabethan secretary letter forms persisted into the late seventeenth century and beyond, so anglicana letter forms persisted into the records of the late sixteenth century.

There are particular challenges involved in reading these records. Some interesting records, such as depositions in ecclesiastical court cases or the records of equity suits, were recorded in English even before the sixteenth century, but most legal documents were written in an abbreviated Latin, which is impenetrable without a good understanding of the marks and symbols that were used. Many letter forms, especially of capital letters, are unrecognisable compared with both modern letter forms and Tudor secretary letter forms. Counter-intuitively, perhaps, records such as manor court rolls written in late seventeenth century and early eighteenth-century court hands, which genealogists may encounter fairly early on in their research, are more difficult to read than those of the fifteenth century; and documents written in fifteenth-century secretary hands may be easier to read than similar Elizabethan records.

EXERCISE 5.1

As you transcribe the following fifteenth-century copy will from the will registers of the Prerogative Court of Canterbury, compare the letter forms with those of the Elizabethan secretary in the copy will from the same source in excerpt g, in Exercise 3.8 in Chapter 3 above. Note that in the latter, the Tudor secretary letters 'r', 'h', 'c' and terminal 's' are distinctive and unlike modern letter forms; here, all of these letters are recognisable from their modern forms, apart from the 'v' form 'r' and the circular 'e'. Typical fifteenth-century secretary letter forms are shown in the first column of Table C.1 in Appendix C.

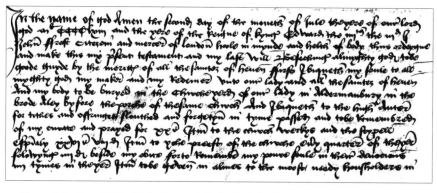

Figure 5.1: Copy Will of John Frost, July 1463. (*The National Archives, ref: PROB 11/5/211*)

Many fifteenth-century hands mixed fifteenth-century secretary and anglicana letter forms.

	Anglicana		Secretary	
a	a		a	
d	d		d	
g	g		g	
r	r		v	2
s	ſ	ſ	ſ	ß
w	w	w	w	

Figure 5.2: Characteristic fifteenth-century small letters forms.

EXERCISE 5.2

Referring to the fifteenth-century letter forms shown in Figure 5.2, transcribe the following letter. Both anglicana and secretary forms of the letters 'a', 'w' and 'r' are used, alongside anglicana 'g' and terminal 's'. Most of the marks of abbreviation are otiose (used ornamentally or through force of habit where they had no purpose).

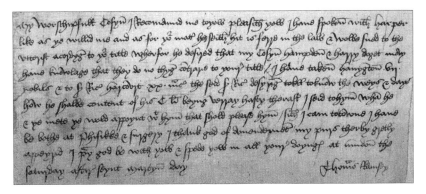

Figure 5.3: Letter from Thomas Ramsey to William Stonor, 12 November 1474. (*The National Archives, ref: SC 1/46/227*)

EXERCISE 5.3

The following two excerpts for transcription are from rent rolls written two centuries apart, the first in the early sixteenth century, the second in the early fourteenth century. The sixteenth-century schedule has a mixture of secretary and anglicana letter forms, while the earlier extent is pure anglicana. The difficulty here is recognising the capital letters in the list of names, particularly the capital letter 'R', and the capital letter 'S', which may easily be mistaken for the letter 'M'.

Figure 5.4

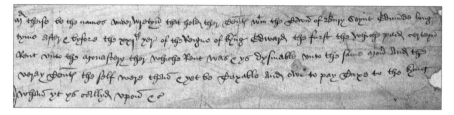

a. **Sixteenth-century Schedule of Holders of Tenements, Bury St Edmunds.** (*The National Archives, ref: SC 12/15/3*)

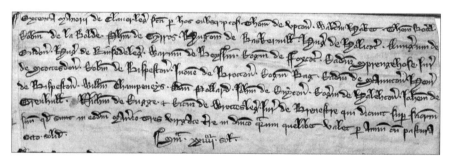

b. **Fourteenth-century Extent for Claverley Manor, Shropshire.** (*The National Archives, ref: SC 12/14/24*)

L.C. Hector traces the evolution of the thirteenth-century business hand and the introduction of 'bastard' and hybrid hands in the fourteenth century, in *The Handwriting of English Documents*. The distinctive small letter forms remained fairly constant from when they first appeared in England in the twelfth century until anglicana was superseded by Tudor secretary in the sixteenth century, apart from the changing fashions for hooks, loops and splits on ascenders. This means that once the anglicana letter forms shown in Table C.2, in Appendix C, are mastered, the very earliest existing records are accessible to the researcher; difficulties are more likely to be caused by the state of preservation of the document, rather than the handwriting.

Anglicana letter forms, especially the letters 'r', 'g' and 'w', are found mixed with secretary well into the sixteenth century, but in general documentary handwriting, even these letters are eventually supplanted by their secretary counterparts. In the central law courts, however, the anglicana letter forms not only survived into the sixteenth century, but developed further into highly distinctive scripts, which by the early eighteenth century are almost illegible at first sight.

Anglicana also survived as a general legal hand and will be found in a variety of documents. In manor court records, it is found alongside secretary and italic – sometimes on the same page – into the eighteenth century.

EXERCISE 5.4

Transcribe and translate the following excerpts, which demonstrate changes in the letter forms of legal hands between the early sixteenth and early eighteenth centuries.

In excerpt a, from a foot of fine made in the Court of Common Pleas in the early sixteenth century, most of the letter forms are now familiar from the earlier anglicana letter forms. Note especially the highly distinctive anglicana 'w', which appeared alongside the secretary 'w' in the letter in Figure 5.3.

Excerpt b, from a mid-sixteenth-century manor court roll, shows some new letter forms. The anglicana letter forms for several capital letters, such as 'H', 'L' and 'M', are identical to the small letter forms, but 'B' needs to be carefully distinguished from the 'D' shown in excerpt a.

In excerpt c, the letters 'c', 'a', terminal 'i', 'r', 'w' and 't', shown here in the words 'coram', 'qui' and 'lostwithiel', all taken from the Memorandum, are quite unlike any forms we have met so far.

  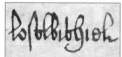

Note the difference between the letters 'g' and 'q', shown here in the words 'antiquus Burgus'.

The final excerpt (d) in Figure 5.5, from an early eighteenth-century court book, shows the influence of the common-law hand on handwriting outside of the central courts, and demonstrates clearly why local court records often prove very difficult to read, especially in the late seventeenth and early eighteenth centuries. Note in particular the tailed 'r', which looks like a cursive 'z', and the final 'i' resembling an open small 'd', already seen in excerpt c. Many local records are only accessible with a good working knowledge of legal hand letter forms.

Figure 5.5: Examples of legal hands from the sixteenth to eighteenth centuries.

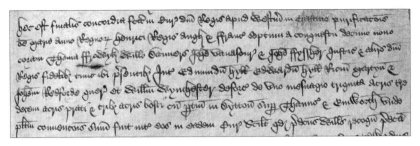

a. Final Concord, early sixteenth century. (*The National Archives, ref: CP 25/1/232/79*)

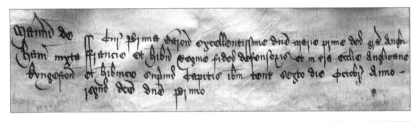

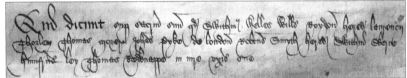

b. Court Roll, Manor of Ham, 1553–54. (*Surrey History Centre, ref: K58/2/1/3*)

c. Memorandum, Files of Indictments, Easter 1728. (*The National Archives, ref: KB 11/29/1728 East*)

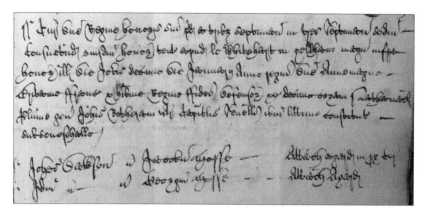

d. Court Book, Clare Honor Manor, 1712. (*The National Archives, ref: DL 30/121/1852. Duchy copyright material in The National Archives is the property of Her Majesty the Queen in Right of Her Duchy of Lancaster. This image is reproduced by permission of the Chancellor and the Council of the Duchy of Lancaster*)

EXERCISE 5.5

The illegibility of the legal hand reached its peak just before court hands were abolished by an Act of Parliament. There is no way of guessing what the following says, without a knowledge of the late forms of the letters 'a', 'c' and 'i'. It is worth familiarising yourself with them, as they turn up regularly in local court records before 1733. The memorandum in Figure 5.5 above should help with the following case of John Purser, a printer and Jacobite sympathiser.

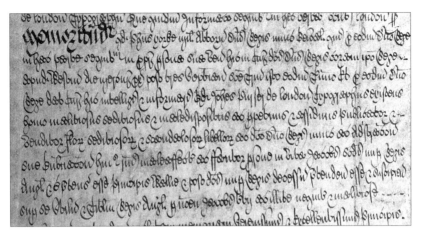

Figure 5.6: Memorandum in King's Bench Crown Roll, 1732. (*The National Archives, ref: KB 28/122*)

'Parliament hand', the Chancery hand used to enrol Acts of Parliament, was the only court hand to survive the general abolition of court hands and became so stylised that by the late eighteenth century, the Parliament Rolls are barely legible. Other enrolments, however, written in Chancery hand with its distinctive round appearance, are easily legible through the sixteenth and seventeenth centuries, and the hand underwent little change.

EXERCISE 5.6

Transcribe the following excerpts, from a selection of Chancery enrolments from the mid-sixteenth century to the early eighteenth century.

Figure 5.7: Examples of Chancery hand from the sixteenth, seventeenth and early eighteenth centuries.

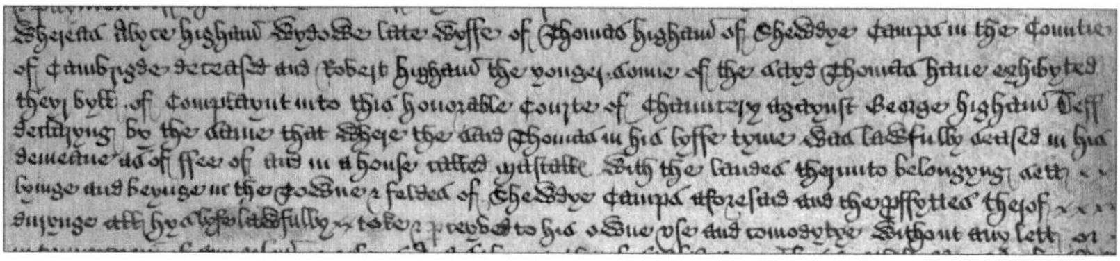

a. Chancery Final Decree, 1562. (*The National Archives, ref: C 78/19/34*)

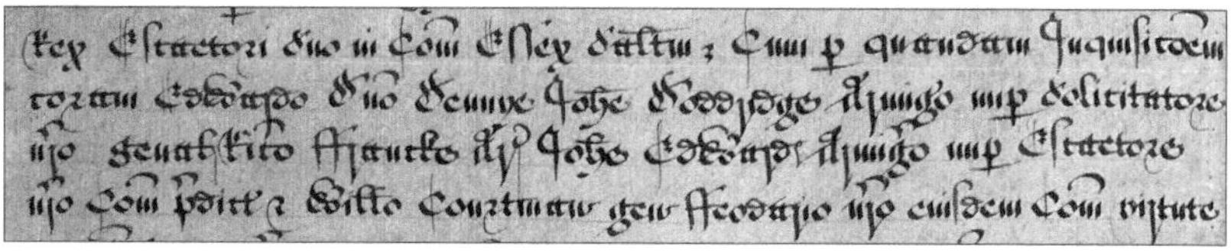

b. Chancery Fine Roll, 1609–10. (*The National Archives, ref: C 60/454/3*)

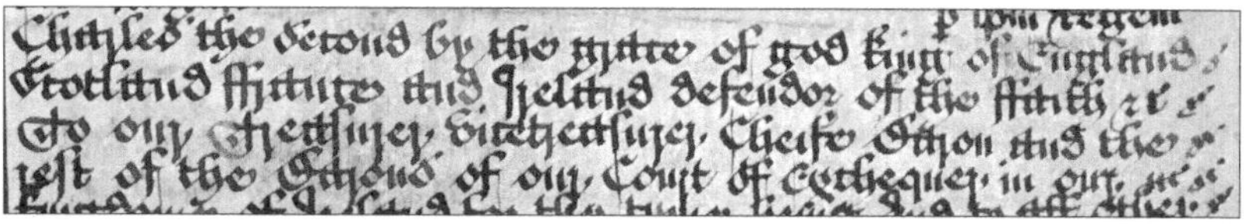

Charles the second by the grace of god king of England
Scotland ffrance and Ireland defender of the faith &c
To our Treasurer Chancellor Chiefe Baron and the
rest of the Barons of our Court of Exchequer in our

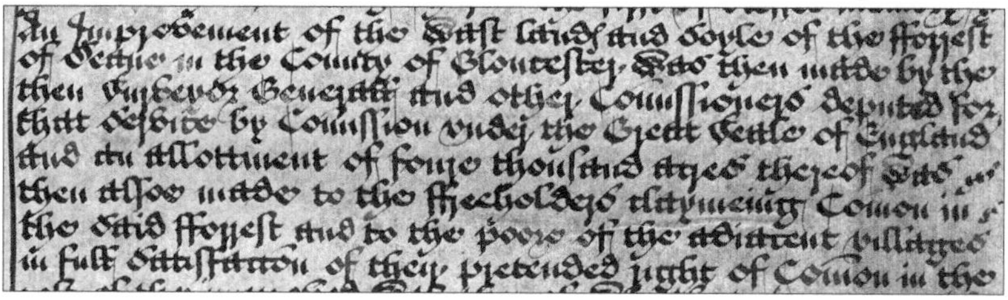

An Improvement of the wast lands and soyle of the fforest
of Dean in the County of Gloucester was then made by the
then Surveyor Generall and other Commissioners deputed for
that service by Commission under the Great Seale of England
and an allottment of foure thousand acres thereof was
then alsoe made to the ffreeholders clayming Comon in
the said fforest and to the poore of the adjacent villages
in full satisfaction of their pretended right of Comon in the

c. Patent Roll, 1667. (*The National Archives, ref: C 66/3088*)

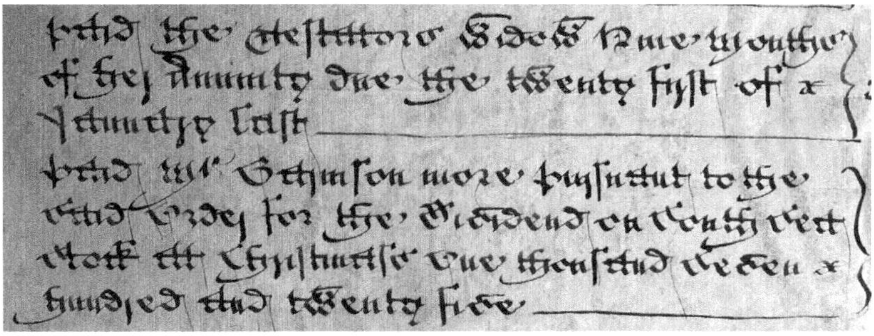

d. Chancery Final Decree, early eighteenth century. (*The National Archives, ref: C 78/1423*)

Final Selections: Excerpts from Records in Court Hands

EXERCISE 5.7

The final selection of records for transcription includes the earliest excerpt yet presented, a thirteenth-century grant of land in Norfolk (excerpt a). Note the split ascenders, with heavy shading on the left fork, typical of this date; the heavy shading, particularly on the 'l', may easily be mistaken for a mark of abbreviation.

Fines, of which the 'foot of fine' was enrolled in the Court of Common Pleas as a record (excerpt b), follow a set form. Read through the 'Final Concord' in the University of Nottingham's 'Manuscripts and Special Collections' web pages before attempting this transcription and translation.

Figure 5.8: Excerpts from records written in court hands.

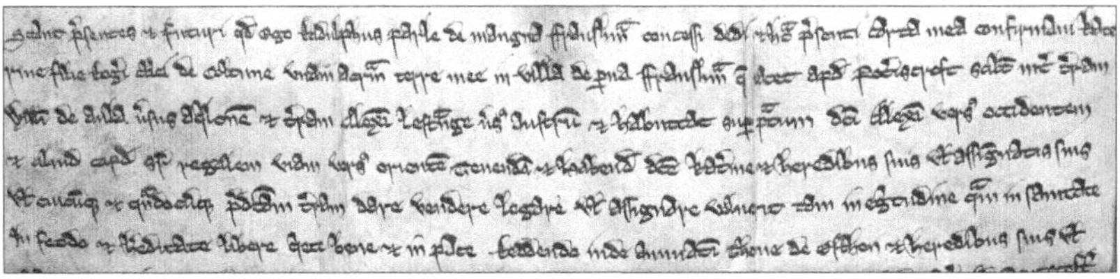

a. Deed, Court of Wards and Liveries, thirteenth century. (*The National Archives, ref: WARD 2/53/179/15*)

b. Final Concord, Surrey Feet of Fines. (*The National Archives, ref: CP 25/2/225/11/12ELIZIMICH*)

Two different set hands were used in the Exchequer, both used in Memoranda Rolls, and both show similarities to other court hands. The Lord Treasurer's Remembrancer's hand, shown in excerpt c, is similar to the hand used in Common Pleas; and the King's Remembrancer's hand, shown in excerpt d, which concerns a woman who was executed for the murder of her husband, is similar to the hand used in Chancery; the alphabets in C.2 will suffice to tackle these. (A third hand, used only for the Pipe Rolls, is also accessible with these alphabets.)

c. Lord Treasurer's Remembrancer's Memoranda Roll, 1633. (*The National Archives, ref: E 368/629*)

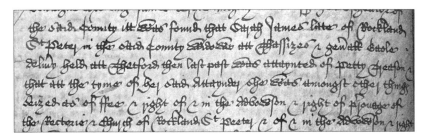

d. King's Remembrancer's Memoranda Roll, 1642. (*The National Archives, ref: E 159/482*)

Excerpts e and f are both taken from local court records and provide good practice reading lists of names. Excerpt g, a letter written in English, contains a range of marks of abbreviation, the yogh and the thorn, and both anglicana and secretary letter forms.

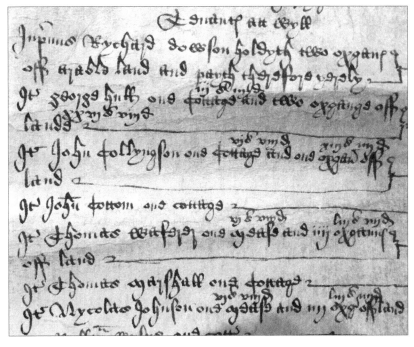

e. Rental, Flamborough Manor, 1550–51. (*The National Archives, ref: SC 11/732*)

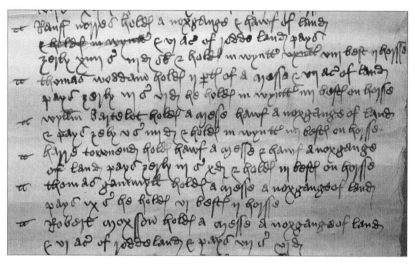

f. Rental, Rothwell Manor, 1528–29. (*The National Archives, ref: SC 11/757*)

g. Letter, William Goldwyn to Agnes Stonor, 18 July 1480. (*The National Archives, ref: SC 1/46/242*)

If you can comfortably read all the final selections in each chapter of this book, you can access the entire range of records in English archives. Nothing can be done about documents that are faded into illegibility or damaged beyond repair, and nothing can be done about the poor handwriting that will be found at every date. However, if you are prepared to work slowly, checking every letter, word by word, even the handwriting in the following excerpt should be legible. It always helps to know what to expect, so check The National Archives' online catalogue; the records of the Court of Wards and Liveries have been expertly catalogued at the item level.

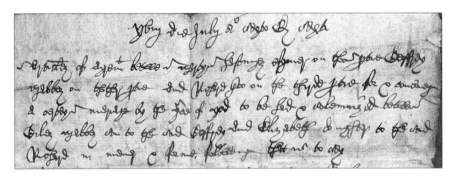

h. Agreement, 1552. (*The National Archives, ref: WARD 2/53/179/98*)

Further Practice and Resources for Reading Records in Court Hands

A handful of publications, which have already been mentioned, are essential when studying medieval Latin records: *The Record Interpreter* by Charles Trice Martin, *Latin for Local History* by Eileen Gooder, *Revised Medieval Latin Word-List from British and Irish Sources* by R.E. Latham, Cheyney's *A Handbook of Dates for Students of British History* and the British Academy's *Dictionary of Medieval Latin from British Sources*.

It should be clear from Exercise 5.2 that the spelling and grammar of records written in middle English may be as challenging to read as those written in Latin. The two-volume *Shorter Oxford English Dictionary*, first published in 1933, is invaluable, along with the six volumes of Wright's *English Dialect Dictionary*, available online through the University of Innsbruck.

Transcription practice is always useful, and there are a number of works with facsimiles and authoritative transcripts. L.C. Hector's *The Handwriting of English Documents* is especially useful, but there are several publications containing facsimiles of medieval records. K.C. Newton's *Medieval Local Records* is useful for a range of early medieval records like the grant in Exercise 5.6 above, and both *Examples of English Handwriting 1150–1750* by Hilda Grieve, and *Palaeography for Family and Local Historians* by Hilary Marshall contain examples of transcriptions and translations of public and private medieval records.

For help with Latin, parallel texts are useful. Selden Society publications, and the *Parliament of Medieval England Rolls*, available at British History Online, both present Latin transcriptions in parallel with an English translation.

For all medieval records, a knowledge of the form of words or the procedure normally employed is key to transcribing a document. Difficulties encountered with one particular document may be overcome by consulting a formulary, such as Hubert Hall's *A Formula Book of English Official Historical Documents*, or studying the form and content of other records in the same collection.

Many local record societies have published visitation records and court books, which are useful for gaining a familiarity with the format and arrangement of administrative and legal documents.

The University of Nottingham website has a guide to identifying and understanding deeds in its *Manuscript and Special Collections* pages. Any serious student of medieval public records will need to consult *English Medieval Diplomatic Practice* by Pierre Chaplais, and Hilary Jenkinson's 1927 volumes on *The Later Court Hands in England, from the Fifteenth Century to the Seventeenth Century*; both are available to view in the library of The National Archives.

A huge range of images of medieval documents is available online. See, for example, the copy wills in the series PROB 11 at The National Archives, and the public records of medieval and early modern England, digitised and displayed on the Anglo-American Legal Tradition website of the O'Quinn Law Library of the University of Houston. Most records, however, still lie unindexed in archives, waiting to be taken up and read for the first time in centuries.

And Finally …

… a selection of five documents, all written in English, to test the entire range of your transcription skills.

First, a nuncupative will from 1628, which was also registered in the Prerogative Court of Canterbury with some further family information. It is written in a typical mixed hand of the period, with several different forms of many letters:

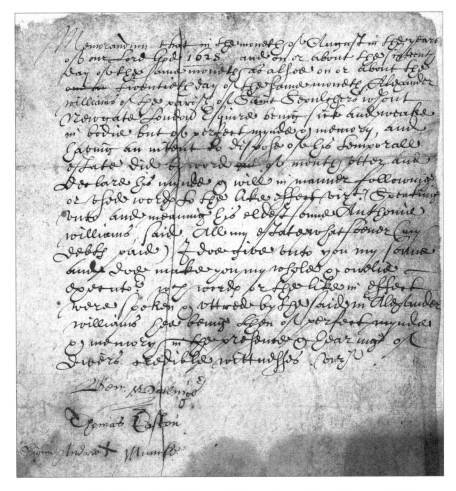

Nuncupative will of Alexander Williams, St Sepulchre's without Newgate, 1628.
(*The National Archives, ref: E 135/24/88*)

A letter summoning Richard Hoo and others to appear before commissioners to be examined on a bill to be heard in Chancery. It is written in a mid-sixteenth-century secretary hand, with a number of abbreviations used in writings in English:

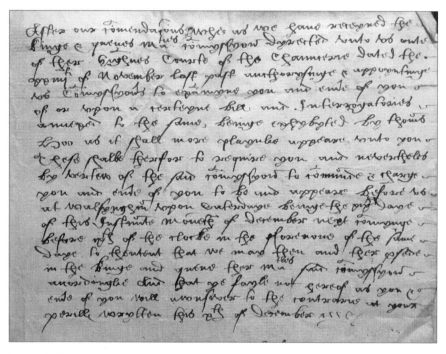

Letter, 10 December 1556. (*The National Archives, ref: WARD 2/53/179/122*)

A letter from a century earlier, employing both secretary ('w') and anglicana ('r', 'a') letter forms. At this date, there is a clear difference between the letter 'y' and the Saxon thorn:

Letter, mid-fifteenth century. (*The National Archives, ref: SC 1/46/248*)

A late sixteenth-century copy of a certificate of the marriage by licence between Francis Wolley and Mary Hawtrie. There are several abbreviations, and unusual letter forms – in particular, the 'b' already encountered in Figure 3.9c:

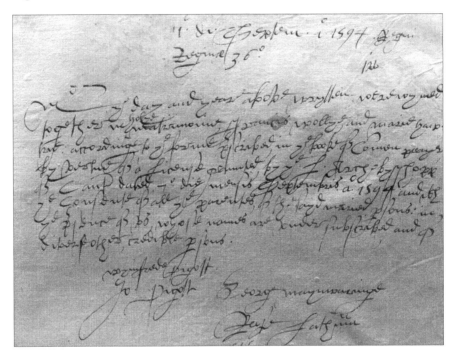

Copy of a marriage certificate, 11 September 1594. (*Surrey History Centre, ref: 6729/7/126. Reproduced by kind permission of the More-Molyneux family and Surrey History Centre*)

The final excerpts continue the articles of agreement of the mid-sixteenth-century marriage settlement recorded in the document in Figure 5.8h. There is a very challenging mix here of anglicana and secretary letter forms, phonetic spelling and a wide range of abbreviations. The initial open 's', the carelessly written anglicana 'w', 'a' and 'v' and the generally poor handwriting mean you are unlikely to come across anything harder to read than this:

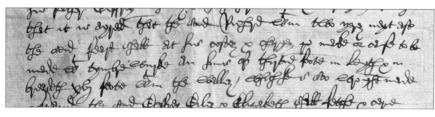

Articles of agreement, 1552. (*The National Archives, ref: WARD 2/53/179/98*)

Answers to Exercises

EXERCISE 1.2

1　All that part of the Parish of Teddington from Broomfield House to the Manor Farm

2　Water Lane, Grove House, and Cottages within the Grove, Teddington Place

3　including the whole of High Street, Meadow Cottage to the North Side of the

4　wax factory

5　Richard Rice, Enumerator.

EXERCISE 1.4

Following the transcription conventions, superior letters are lowered, words are expanded within square brackets, and line fillers are ignored.

　'Do' is written here for 'ditto', without a sign of abbreviation, and is commonly used in lists to avoid repetition. 'Instant' means the current month, i.e. January.

		Baptisms Jan[uar]y 1800	S[u]r Names	Born
1	1	Mary D[aughte]r of Will[ia]m [and] Ann	Dennis	6 Dec[embe]r Last
2	3	Sarah D[aughte]r Will[ia]m Eliz[abe]th	Birkwood	11 D[itt]o
3	5	George Son George Ann	Moss	7 D[itt]o
4	12	George Son George Eliz[abe]th	Chambers	17 D[itt]o
5	12	Tho[ma]s Son Tho[ma]s Mary	Jones	12 D[itt]o
6	12	George Son Eliz[abe]th	Russell	
7	19	John Son David Eliz[abe]th	Matthews	27 Nov[embe]r Last
8	26	John Son Tho[ma]s Ann	Golding	4 Ins[tan]t
9	27	Henry Son Zachariah Susannah	Hawkins	27 Dec[embe]r 99
10	29	Tho[ma]s Son Charles Ann	Farbrother	19 D[itt]o Last
11	31	Martha D[aughte]r Sarah	Townsend	11 Ins[tan]t

EXERCISE 1.5

Following the transcriptions conventions, the Saxon thorn, which looks like a 'y' in line 2, is silently replaced with 'th'; capital letters and small letters are retained throughout; and editorial notes are footnoted underneath the transcription.

		£	s	d
1	A tru Imnetary of goods and Chattels			
2	of william Iles of the parish of			
3	Beitton in the Countty of Gloussestor			
4	Apart in a Cotage hous	10	10	00
5	and a Clock	1	5	00
6	and peuter[1] and Bras and [and][2] Iron	1	0	00
7	and two beds [and] other lumbord[3] goods	1	10	00
8	and half acer of Ground	2	10	00
9		16	15	00
10	praised[4] by Samuel brain			
11	and michel Iles Witness our hand			

[1] *Pewter*

[2] *Superfluous ampersand*

[3] *Lumber: disused articles of furniture*

[4] *Appraised: priced or valued*

EXERCISE 1.6

a.

1 Whereas Mary Farrer of Midgley singlewoman hath th[i]s
2 day come before me [and] taken her corporall Oath that about 30
3 weeks agoe, David Megson of the same towne did begett a child
4 on her body w[hi]ch child when born will be a bastard, and likely
5 to be chargeable to the parish; and that he is the sole father of the same
6 These are therefore in his Maj[es]ties name to charge [and] comand
7 you or some of you to attach the body of the said David Megson and
8 bring him before me or some others of his Maj[es]ties Justices of the peace
9 for this Riding p[ro]vided with two sufficient suretys for his {personell}
10 appearance at the next Generall Quarter Sessions of the peace to be
11 holden at <...> ^Wakefield^ for this Rideing, and there Receive such further
12 orders as that court shall think p[ro]per, Herein fail not etc. Given
13 under my hand [and] seal at Calverley the 7th of October Annoq[ue] Dom[in]i 1718

b.

Dorsetshire

1 The Examination[1] of Benj[amin] Miller now Residing in the parish of
2 Melbury Osmond in the s[ai]d County Labourer Taken on his
3 Oath before us Two of his Majesties Justices of the

4   Peace for the said County the 13th day of December 1752
5   Concerning the place of his settlem[en]t
6   Who saith that he was Born in the s[ai]d parish of Melbury
7   Osmond as he hath been Informed and believes That he
8   went when he was ab[ou]t Fourteen years of age and hired
9   himself by the week to Tho[ma]s Deering late of Chetnole in the
10   said County for a shilling a week and his Victualls and {…}
11   Lodging Except Sundays when he dined at his fathers That
12   He lived under that contract for <…> half a year <…> or there
13   abouts That he returned home from thence and went and
14   Lived at Melbury Osmond af[ore]s[ai]d and there Married where he hath
15   ever since Lived and worked as a Labourer And saith that
16   he hath done no <…> act to gain a settlement other than as
17   afores[ai]d

[1] *It is often difficult, as here, to determine the intent of the writer when capital letters take a similar form to small letters*

EXERCISE 1.7

a.

1   One pole and Six Feet lying and being in the parish of Ugley in the County of Essex
     aforesaid
2   On the Seventeenth day of March in the Second Year of the Reign of our Sovereign
     Lord George
3   the Third now King of great Britain etc and continually afterwards Until the day of the
     taking
4   of this Inquisition at the parish aforesaid in the County aforesaid was and now is very
     Ruinous
5   miry deep founderous and in Such decay for Want of due reparation and Amendment
     of the
6   Same So that the Leige Subjects of Our said Lord the King by the Same way with their
     Horses
7   Carts and Carriages by the whole time aforesaid could not nor now can go return pass
     ride and
8   labour as they were wont and ought to do without great danger of their Lives and the
     Loss
     of their Goods To the great damage and Common Nusance of all the Leige Subjects of
     our
9   said Lord the King …

b.
1　　Boundaries
2　　Thames Bank from Opposite Cleaveland Road
3　　to the boundary of Kingston and Long Ditton
4　　Parishes, Parish Boundary to Balaclava Road,
5　　West side of Balaclava Road and Maple Road,
6　　to Cleaveland Road, South side of Cleaveland
7　　Road to the River Thames Bank

c.
1　　Thomas and nancy Son and
2　　Daughter of Samuel and Ann
3　　Mores was Baptized the
4　　the[1] 17 day of July 1785
5　　Sarah Daughter of John and
6　　Mary Almes was Baptized
7　　the 21 day of Aug[us]t 1785
8　　Jane the Daughter of George
9　　and Jane Price was Baptized
10　 the 28 day of Aug[us]t 1785
11　 Ric[hard] the son of Ric[har]d and
12　 Sarah Gough was Baptized
13　 25 day of Sep[tembe]r 1785

[1] 'the' is repeated

d.
1　　Signed sealed published [and] Declared by the
2　　said William Barnes the Testator to be his
3　　last Will [and] Testament in the pr[e]sence of us
4　　whose names are hereunto subscribed as
5　　Witnesses [and] attested by us as such in the
6　　pr[e]sence of the said Testator.

e. Following the transcription conventions, all spellings are retained, and the definitions of
　 unfamiliar words are then footnoted:

1　　Imprimise wearing Aparrell and Money in purss
2　　Four Cow Beast
3　　Two Earlin[1] Beast
4　　five Hors flesh
5　　11 Acres and half of Wheat growing
6　　Wheat in the Barn 25 bushells at 8s p[er] bush[el]
7　　Beans in the Barn and House 50 bushells at 4s p[er] bush[el]
8　　one Fatt pigg

9   Horses Geers of all Sorts
10   one Sadle and one pad
11   one Wagon and one Carte
12   Harrows and dray and plow

[1] *Yearling*

f.
1   A Inventory of the goods [and] Chattels of samywell davis
2   late of the parish of horsly In the County of Glosestur
3   free masen deceased Tacken [and] a praised by
4   us whose namse are hear unto subscribed the 10 day

	£	s	d
5 of July ^in 1735^			
6 imprimis: the testaters waring aparel [and] muny in pus	2	1	3
7 imprimis: for pewltur [and] brase [and] lumbur goods	3	0	0
8 imprimse: for 3 ornury bedse [and] bedse steeds won	2	3	2
9 Chust [and] a box[1]			

[1] *Lines 8 and 9: 'for three ordinary beds and bedsteads, one chest and a box'*

EXERCISE 2.1

Following the transcription conventions, 'li' for 'libras' (here, Latin accusative plural, meaning 'pounds') is not expanded, but the familiar £ sign is used. Deletions are enclosed within angle brackets, with text supplied.

1   Spernall October the 26th 1696
2   A true list of all persons inhabiting w[i]thin
3   the said p[ar]ish who have within this County
4   £10 p[er] ann[um] [and] upward in lands tenem[en]ts or rents
5   in fee simple fee tayle coppy hold or for
6   life
7   Thomas Price: <hath> yeoman <hath> aged about
8   53 yeares: he hath about £30 p[er] annu[m] in free
9   hold [and] long leases: soe entangled in morgages [and]
10   otherwise that not long since he swore himselfe
11   not worth £10
12   Edward Gale yeoman hath an estate for his
13   life about the value of £20 p[er] annu[m] he is aged
14   about 63 yeares: And soe infirme in body by
15   reason of a rupture that he hath not bin able
16   to travell 5 miles from home for some yeares
17   last past
18   There is noe other person within the said p[ar]ish
19   that hath any such estate of £10 p[er] annu[m] as aboves[ai]d

EXERCISE 2.2

1   John Compton in another house w[hi]ch lyes desolate
2   John Perkins
3   Johnson Higges
4   Richard Kench
5   Mathew Newton
6   Katherine Gamble widd[ow]
7   Basill Feilding Esq[ui]r[e]
8   William Warde
9   William Hancox
10 Engram Dafforne
11 Reede widd[ow]
12 Thomas Onely
13 Henry Gibson
14 Uziah Atkins
15 Humfrey Danes
16 Katherine Querne

EXERCISE 2.3

a.

1   Signed and Sealed by the
2   Churchwarden [and] Overseere
3   of Latton in the pr[e]sence
4   of Michael[1] Altham vicar

[1] *The mark through the ascender of 'h' in 'Michael' has no abbreviative purpose*

b.

Following the transcription conventions, the line fillers at the end of lines 1 and 3 do not form part of the transcription.

1   The Condic[i]on of this obligac[i]on is such, That whereas Joan Pickett
2   single-woman was lately gotten with Child by the above bounden
3   Robert Bridgeman, as appeares as well by the accusac[i]on of the

c.

1   In obedience to your Hon[ou]rs Com[m]and In yours bearing
2   date 15th [Decem]ber. I was with M[aste]r Mason as soone as

d.

1   Know all men by these pr[e]sents

e.

1   this Case made [and] p[ro]vyded

f.

2   [Christoph]er Sharpe

g.

1   whereas yo[u]r pet[itione]r being a porter [and] hath noe manner of livelyhood but God[es]
2   blessing upon his Indeavours to support or comfort himself [and] 3 small
3   Motherlesse Children whose crying want[es] requyre continuall
4   supply

h.

vi[delicet] for the stealing

EXERCISE 2.4

a.

1   Chatham 24[th]
2   Jann[ua]r[y] 1676/7

(24 January 1677)

b.

1   Memorand[um] quod decimo quinto die decembris An[n]o Regni dom[ini] no[st]ri Car[oli] s[e]c[un]di dei gratia
2   Anglie Scotie Francie et Hibernia[1] Regis fidei defensor[is] etc decimo quarto

[1] *Should be 'Hibernie'*

Translation:
Memorandum that on the fifteenth day of December in the fourteenth year of the reign of our Lord Charles II by the grace of God king of England, Scotland, France and Ireland, defender of the faith etc.

(Using table 2/II in Cheney's *Handbook of Dates*, 15 December in the fourteenth year of the reign of Charles II falls in the year 1662, so the date is 15 December 1662.)

c.

1   … decimo septimo die Martii Anno
2   R[egni] R[eginae] Annae dei gratia Angl[iae] etc quarto Annoq[ue] D[omi]ni 1704

Translation:
On the seventeenth day of March in the fourth year of the reign of Anne by grace of God queen of England etc and in the year of the lord 1704.

Note the 'ae' digraph, which is very common at this date in place of the medieval 'e'.

EXERCISE 2.5

1   Whereas the Court was moved by Councell on the behalfe of the parish of Houlgate
2   in this County as also by petic[i]on from the Churchwardens and overseers of the
3   poore of the said parish that one Edmund Dixon a Blacksmith and his wife are
4   unduely put upon their parish to provide for them whereas the said parishoners
5   Doubt not but to make it cleerly appeare that by him they ought to bee p[ro]vided
6   for in the parish of Clee St Margarets in the the said County where the said <depon[en]t>
7   Dixon was duely settled untill his house there after the said {...} was illegally
8   pulled Downe. It is therefore ordered by the Court that notwithstanding any former
9   Ord[e]rs made at the Quarter Sessions of the peace the said settlem[en]t bee duely Examined
10 betweene the said parishes by Edward B<ald>awdwyn and Charles Bawldwin Esq[uire]rs
11 Justices of the peace neare adjoineing who are desired to call all p[ar]ties concerned
12 before them and to make such ord[e]r therein upon ^the^ truth of the fact on both sides as
13 shalbee agreeable to law or in case they cannot satifie the said parishes therein
14 to certefie the matter of fact to the Justices of Assize at the next Assize held for
15 this County that a finall ord[e]r may bee had therein And that some of Both parishes
16 Doe attend the Court thereupon

EXERCISE 2.7

a.

1   September
2   The 2nd Margaret Selfe Widow
3   The 1st John fil[iu]s Richard[1] Sadler
4   The 4th Robert fil[iu]s Tho[mas] Harding of Barrotts Bridge
5   The 8th Thomas Wayt senior
6   The 11th Sarah ux[or] Daniel Bocky
7   The 17th Daniel Bocky
8   The 18th John fil[iu]s Matthew Collier
9   The 20th Joseph fil[iu]s Anthony Archer

[1] *Although the register is in Latin, forenames as well as surnames are written in English. This is not usually the case*

b.

1   Johannes Barwis Admissus est Tenens Unius Messuag[ii] et
2   Ten[emen]ti cum p[er]tinentiis Scituat[i] et Iacent[is] in Newcowp[er] Annual[em]
3   Reddit[um] xxˢ Tenendum sibi et heredib[us] suis imp[er]petuum
4   S[e]c[un]d[u]m consuetud[inem] Mannerii p[re]dicti, Ex Sursum reddic[i]one
5   Roberti Barwis patris sui, Et dat pro Fine suo -

Translation:

John Barwis was admitted tenant of one messuage and tenement with appurtenances situated and lying in New Cowper [at] annual rent of 20s to hold to him and his heirs for ever according to the custom of the aforesaid manor, by surrender of Robert Barwis his father. And he gives for his fine -

c.

1 Nov[er]int univ[er]si p[er] pr[e]sentes nos Rob[er]tum Bridgeman de p[ar]och[ia]
2 de Enfield in Com[itatu] Midd[lese]x[ie] yeom[an] [et] Thoma[m] Bridgeman sen[iorem]
3 de p[ar]ochia [et] Com[itatu] pr[e]d[ictis] yeom[an]
4 ten[er]i et firmit[er] obligari Joh[ann]i Lullock, Franc[isc]o White, et Will[elm]o
5 Bignall yeo[men] Guardian[is] Ecclesiae p[ar]och[ie] de Enfield pr[e]dict[a] in Centu[m]
6 libris bone [et] legalis monet[e] angl[ie] solvend[is] eisdem Joh[ann]i Lullock
7 Franc[isc]o White, [et] Will[elm]o Bignall [et] eor[u]m successor[ibus], ad quam
8 quidem soluc[i]one[m] bene et fidelit[er] faciend[am] obligam[us] nos [et] utrumq[ue]
9 n[ost]ru[m] p[er] se p[ro] toto [et] in solid[o] heredes exec[uto]res [et] adm[inistrato]res n[ost]ros firmit[er]
10 p[er] pr[e]sentes sigillis n[ost]ris sigillat[as] Dat[um] …

Translation:

Know all men by these presents that we Robert Bridgeman of the parish of Enfield in the county of Middlesex yeoman and Thomas Bridgeman the elder of the aforesaid parish and county, are held and firmly bound to John Lullock, Francis White and William Bignall, yeomen, guardians of the parish church of Enfield aforesaid, in one hundred pounds of good and legal money of England to be paid to the same John Lullock, Francis White and William Bignall, and to their successors; for which payment to be well and faithfully made we bind ourselves, and each of us by himself for the whole and jointly, our heirs, executors, administrators, firmly by these presents, sealed with our seals. Dated [as Exercise 2.4c]

d.

1 Soe it is That one Baldridge a Bailiff having extreamly Injured and
2 damnified the pet[itione]r by his fraudulent dealing, <…> [and] thereupon the pet[itione]r
3 was promised an Indictem[en]t ag[ains]t him, and now the Clerk deferrs the
4 framing thereof on purpose to drive the pet[itione]r from any releifs or
5 Justice till next Sessions.

e.

1 11° die Aprilis 1683
2 Cottagium sive Ten[emen]tu[m] suu[m] Customar[ium] cum suis app[er]tinen[ciis][1] Scituat[um] iacen[s]
3 et existen[s] in p[ar]ochia de Twickenham in Com[itatu] Midd[lese]x[ie] int[e]r terra[m] Will[ielm]i
4 Baker juni[oris] ex Oriental[i] et Heredes[2] Ric[ard]i Rayner ex occidental[i] et
5 Austral[i] Ad solu[m] p[ro]p[r]iu[m] opus et usu[m] pr[e]d[i]c[t]i Will[ielm]i Baker Jun[ioris] de

6   Petworth in Com[itatu] Sussex[ie] Gardiner Heredu[m] et Assignat[orum] Suor[um]
7   imp[er]petuu[m] Qui pr[e]sens hic in Cur[ia] petit se admitti inde Tenen[tem] Cui
8   D[omi]nus p[er] Deputat[um] Senescallu[m] suum Concessit inde Sei[sin]am p[er]
     virg[am]
9   Habend[um] et Tenend[um] D[i]c[t]o Will[ielm]o Baker Jun[iori] Hered[ibus] et
     Assignat[is]
10   suis imp[er]petuu[m] ad voluntate[m] D[omi]ni s[e]c[un]d[u]m consuetud[inem]
     Man[er]ii pr[e]d[i]c[t]i p[er]
11   Reddit[us] Consuetud[ines] et Servic[ia] inde prius debit[a] et de iure consuet[a]
12   dat D[omi]no de fine et Heriot[o] inde ii s Et Admissus est inde tenens

[1] *The Latin word 'pertinencia' has been confused with its English translation*
[2] *This should be 'heredum'*

Translation:

On the eleventh day of April 1683

A cottage or customary tenement with its appurtenances situated lying and being in the parish of Twickenham in the county of Middlesex, between the lands of William Baker junior on the east and of the heirs of Richard Rayner on the west and south, to the sole use and benefit of the aforesaid William Baker junior of Petworth in the county of Sussex, gardener, his heirs and assigns for ever, who, being present in court, seeks to be admitted as tenant therein. To whom the lord, by his deputy steward, granted seisin therein by the rod, to have and to hold to the said William Baker junior his heirs and assigns for ever at the will of the lord according to the custom of the aforesaid manor, by rents, customs, and services formerly owed therein, and by right accustomed. He gives two shillings to the lord as fine and heriot in respect thereof. And he was admitted tenant therein.

f.
1   Know all men by these pr[e]sents that I Francis Randall of the
2   parish of Seale in the County of Kent yeoman am held [and] firmly
3   bound unto Richard Patridge Brasier [and] Ralph Palmer Victualler
4   Churchwardens of the parish of St Peters Cornhill London
5   in Fifty pounds of lawfull money of England to be paid to the
6   said Richard Patridge and Ralph Palmer or either of them

g.
1   Att this Court it is found by the homage that on the
2   30th daie of September last past John Cheesman
3   of Hampton upon Thames in the County of Midd[lesex]
4   Fisherman did surrender in to the hand[es] of the lord
5   of this Honor[1] Manor by the roll by the hand[es]
6   and acceptance of Thomas Redknapp [and] Richard
7   Blanchett two Customary Tenants of the said honor
8   and Manor. All that his Acre of arrable land ...

[1] *Hampton Court was created an 'Honour' by Act of Parliament in 1539. Several manors were attached to it under one lord, the Lieutenant and Keeper of the Chase*

EXERCISE 3.1

howse Petworth plac[es]

Lawrence nighte

EXERCISE 3.2

1   And whereas yo[u]r Lo[rdship] doth require to be adv[er]tised
2   from me of som[m]e fitte place betwene my howse and Cowdrey
3   for her ma[jes]tie to lodge in one nighte yt maie please you to
4   understande that ther is not anie convenient howse for that
5   purpose standinge neer the way from my howse towardes
6   Petworth or Cowdrey. Onlie ther is a litle howse of M[aste]r
7   Lawrence Elliot[es] distant three myles from myne the direct
8   waie toward[es] either of the said plac[es] and w[i]thin tenne myles
9   of Petworth and eleaven of Cowdrey to w[hi]ch howse I directed
10 M[aste]r Constable by a servaunt of myne whoe hath viewed the
11 same and canne make reporte to yo[u]r Lo[rdship] thereof From thence
12 ther is another the like howse in Shillinglie of one Bonners
13 distant five myles the direct way to Petworth and about
14 a myle out of the waie to Cowdrey where Kinge Edwarde
15 dyned in his waye from Guildford parke to Cowdrey

EXERCISE 3.3

a.
1   In the name of god amen the 10th day of the moneth of Nove[m]ber
2   In the yeare of o[u]r Lord god 1573 And in the fiftenth yeare of the Reigne
3   of o[u]r sovereigne Ladie Quene Elizabeth I Robert Teisdale of Walsoken
4   w[i]thin the Dioceis of Norwich being sick [and] weake in bodie but whole
5   in mind and of good and p[er]fect reme[m]brance (thank[es] be to Almightie god) Do
6   ordeine [and] make this my testame[n]t conteyning therin my last will in ma[nner]
7   [and] forme folowing

b.
1   I Elene Prat Sycke in bodye and hole
2   of mynde make my testament in this man[ner]
3   Awyse Fyrste I bequethe my Sowle unto
4   all myghtye god my bodye to be buryed
5   in the Chauncell of Inglesham' by my husband

c.
1   … I be queth to
2   o[u]r mother Church of Well[es] 4d It[em] to my p[ar]ysh church of of crukern[1]

3   6s 8d It[em] to the hygh alter 12d It[em] to my sone George my
4   standing cuppe of sylver w[i]th the cover [and] halfe a dosin silv[er] spownes

[1] *'of' is repeated; Crewkerne*

d.
1   It[e]m I will dorothe Smythson mye dafter to be mye
2   sole executryx of this mye Laste will, and Roberte
3   Coleman [and] williame my son[ne] to be the oversears of
4   the same, and the said Robarte coleman to have a
5   blacke gowne for his paynes

e.
1   Probatu[m] fuit h[uius]mo[d]i testamentu[m] cora[m] mag[ist]ro
2   Henrico Joanes legum doctore Surr[ogato] etc xviij°
3   die mens[i]s Julii 1570 iuramento Agnetis
4   eius Relicte et executricis etc Cui comissa
5   fuit Ad[ministraci]o etc de bene etc iurate etc Salvo
6   iure cuiuscu[m]q[ue]

Translation:
This will was proved before Master Henry Joanes, Doctor of laws, surrogate etc, on the eighteenth day of the month of July 1570 by the oath of Agnes, his widow and executrix etc, to whom administration was granted etc,[1] being sworn etc,[2] reserving the rights of all others

[1] *'Etc' covers the phrase 'of all and singular the goods, rights and credits of the deceased'*
[2] *'Etc' covers the phrase 'to well and faithfully administer the same'. These are rarely written out in full in probate clauses*

EXERCISE 3.4.

a.
1   wase baptized
2   dorothe hopkins[1] the
3   daughter of John
4   hopkin[es]
5   wase baptized John
6   Thomson the sonne
7   of william Thomson
8   wase baptized Margret
9   Jones the daughter
10   of rychard Jones

[1] *Indexed online as Arothe Yopltias!*

b.

1	1 John hickoxe the sonne
2	of morrysse hickoxe
3	4 Anna Locke the daugh
4	ter of John Locke
5	23 henry hewlet the sonne
6	of Elyas hewlett
7	1595 Februarye
8	2 Dorathe wyndover the daugh
9	ter of John wyndover
10	2 Elizabeth morsse the daugh
11	ter of henry morsse
12	4 Wyllyam Osburne the sonne
13	of John Osburne

c.

1	John Grafton Clothyer
2	Margerye d[aughter] to Ambrose Barratt
3	Elsabeth d[aughter] to Wyllyam Jeffrye
4	John sonne to morrysse Gauntlett
5	Edward sonne to Richard Ottes
6	Elsabeth wyf to Gyles Turbervell
7	Richard Raye weaver

d.

1	John Haytter a stranger
2	marye d[aughter] to [Christ]ofer Phillips
3	James Sweetappell a smythe

e.

1	July 1610
2	John Nicholls and Sibbell Mason maried the firste daie
3	John Craston and Joane Hewes maried the third daie
4	William Reeve and Eliz[abeth] Pynner maried the eight daie
5	George Vininge and Abigall Jobe the twelveth daie
6	Robert Sayer and Mary Taylor maried the fiftenth daie
7	Nicholas Evans and Dorathie Hunte the sixtenth daie
8	Barnard Garter [and] Marga[ret] Hannam al[ia]s Triplett the 18th daie
9	Zachry Higg[es] and Grace Gatward maried the 23th[1] daie
10	Henrie Richardsone and Eliz[abeth] Smyth maried the 27th daie
11	Frauncis Hewson and Joane Smyth the 30th daie

[1] *Written to be read as 'third and twentieth'*

f.

1   Aprill 11 Alice Chrichell was buried
2   Aprill 21 Deanes Baker was buried
3   May 22 Joane Addams was buried
4   June 19 Robert Perrett was buried
5   August 29 John Oake was buried
6   September 30 Julyan Evans was buried
7   November 10 Peter Gibbens was buried
8   November 17 William Holmead was buried

Almost every entry in the whole of the sixteenth-century part of the register is incorrectly transcribed in Ancestry's online index.

EXERCISE 3.5

a.

1   Inprimis one standinge bedsted
2   It[e]m one Settlebedd w[i]th old lumber
3   It[e]m one wainskott Chest
4   It[e]m one litle table [and] Carpett
5   It[e]m 26[ty][1] pec[es] of Lynnen
6   It[e]m one pursse w[i]th silke buttons
7   It[e]m one Straw bed [and] straw bolster
8   It[e]m a hap harlott w[i]th a fether pillow
9   It[e]m one paire of litle Skales

[1] *Written to be read as 'six and twenty'*

b.

1   P[ai]d For to[1] Busshell of Baie Sallte
2   P[ai]d For thre Sixe Bushell Sack[es]
3   P[ai]d For to half quarter Sack[es]
4   P[ai]d for Coostom Wharffidge [and] the Barge
5   P[ai]d For a paire of Sleves For yo[u]r Self

[1] *Two*

c.

1   It[e]m hire beste Frocke
2   It[em] on othere Frocke
3   It[e]m on worsted certylle[1]
4   It[e]m on Redde petycotte
5   It[em] all hire lynyn
6   It[em] on wastcot of Fusion and
7   on payr of fustyon sleves

8   It[e]m on womans cappe
9   It[e]m on worsted aporne[2]
10   It[em] <3> 2 petycotis

[1] *Kirtle*
[2] *Apron*

d.
1   It[e]m on ex on bylle 2 eyrn wegys – 2s 4d
2   It[e]m 2 huchys – 3s 4d
3   It[e]m on table on Form on p[air] of trestels on Round table – 6s 8d

Item one axe, one bill, two iron wedges
Item two hutches
Item one table, one form, one pair of trestles, one round table

EXERCISE 3.6

a.
1   After my hartie Comendacions I have receaved yo[u]r l[ett]re
2   of the 4 of this instant …

1   Wherin I praie yow take present order. And so I
2   bid yow verie hartelie farewell from my howse att
3   Deptford the 5 daie of November 1595

b.
1   After o[u]r harty co[m]mendac[i]ones, according to yo[u]r l[ett]res lately wryten
2   unto us we have p[ro]cured from the L[ord] Kep[er] of the greate
3   Seale a co[m]mission of Oyer and terminer whereby you
4   maye p[ro]cede to tharreignement[1] of the three p[er]sons who
5   lately co[m]mytted the Roberye and murdre uppon the man
6   of Walton Uppon Themys. The co[m]mission ye shal
7   receyve her w[i]th[2]. We thinke mete, and so is thopinion[3]
8   of my L[ord] Kep[er], that albeyt the co[m]mission be gen[er]all
9   you do nevertheles forbeare to delyv[er] thole[4] gaole
10   but that in p[ro]ceding only agaynst the three p[er]sons
11   named in yo[u]r L[ett]res unto us ye cause the rest
12   to remayn in gaole to receyve their tryal at
13   the co[m]meng thither of the Justic[es] of assise
14   Thus fare you hartely wel From Wyndsor Castle
15   the 26th of february 1563

[1] *'the arraignment'*
[2] *'herewith'*
[3] *'the opinion'*
[4] *'the whole'*

c.

1   M[aste]r Moore und[e]rstanding th[a]t my verey good Lord the Vycount
2   Montague hathe putt one Shorter his s[erv]unt in tryst to
3   have Care of the Que[e]ns Ma[jes]t[ies] game in his Absence in
4   the chasse [and] owt borders of the Forest wherof his L[ordship]
5   hathe charge And p[er]ceyving th[a]t the sayd Shorter hath
6   not well behaved him Self in his charge for p[re]servac[i]on
7   of the same Game Butt rether hathe bene A spoyler
8   [and] dystroyer of the Same As well in the place where
9   he is charged As also in the Forest …

1   And to Certefye me the Cyrcumstance of yo[u]r doing[es]
2   therin w[i]th as muche spede as you can th[a]t I maye
3   take order therin in Suche Sorte As the cays shall
4   Requyer. And so w[i]th my hartie Comendac[i]ons unto
5   you I byd you fayrewell Att the Cowrt att
6   Rychemonde the 5th of August 1565

EXERCISE 3.7

a. the v day of August In the yere of our lord god m ccccc xliij

(5 August 1543)

b.

1   … the Twentie Daie of Maye In the yeare of our
2   Lorde god one Thowsand Five hundred threescore
3   and fowerteene

(20 May 1574)

c.

1   In the name of god Amen The 30th
2   daye of October in the yere of oure Lorde
3   god 1571 the 13th yere of the Reigne of oure
4   Sov[er]aigne Ladye Quene Elizabeth etc

(30 October 1571)

EXERCISE 3.8

a.

1   Edward Shellye ^indyted^ of worminghurste yn

2   the Countye of Sussexe gent[leman]

3   Christofer Archare of the p[ar]ishe of S[ain]t

4   Michaels in Cornwale London gent[leman]

5   Will[ia]m Stapletone of the p[ar]ishe of Bradleye

6   yn the Countye of Stafforde gent[leman]

7   John[1] Bradstocke ^indyted^ of Queene hill in the

8   p[ar]ishe of Rippule yn the Countye of Worcester yeman

9   Jane Goldwyer ^indyted^ Late of Whateleye yn the

10   Countye of Oxforde widowe

[1] *There is an otiose mark of abbreviation here, carried over from the common abbreviation of 'Johannes' in Latin, although the name is not abbreviated in English*

b.

1   In the small p[ar]ishes [and] villag[es] nye to london and

2   specyally in Mydlesex so[m]me of the p[ar]ishes have

3   adventured in Companyes puttyng into the

4   lottery ev[er]y Man According to ther abillytye

5   Some one lott or mo[1] some half a lott so[m]me

6   2s 6d some 12d so[m]me 4d so[m]me 2d or more

7   or lesse According to ther haviours and power

8   and the same is put into the lottery under one

9   posye[2] in the name of the hole p[ar]ishe

[1] *More*

[2] *Posse: a number of people*

c.

1   High Streete

2   Impr[imi]s of the Lady Lister for tenem[en]t[es] in the high Streete

3   late Peters Crewes p[ar]cell of the whitehorse late John Cowpland[es]

4   It[e]m of the heires of M[ist]r[es]s Watson paid by M[aste]r Johnson for

5   land[es] late Nicholas Wilkins

6   It[e]m of M[aste]r John Rawson for a Tenem[en]t late John Gregories land[es]

7   It[e]m of M[aste]r Robert Berrier [and] M[aste]r Leon[ar]d Scott for land[es] late

8   Thomas Daltons

9   It[e]m of M[ist]r[es]s Metcalfe for a Tenem[en]t late Thomas Hodsons

10   It[e]m of the heires of Allexand[e]r Stockdale for one tenem[en]t there late

11   In thoccupac[i]on of Will[ia]m Chamb[e]rs [and] now of Will[ia]m Thompson

d.

1   Richard Whalley s[er]vaunte to Ric[hard] Whalley Esquier of Welbeck in

2   the Countie of Nott[inghamshire] of thage of fortie yeres or thereabout[es] sworne

3   and examyned before Will[ia]m Homberston and Will[ia]m Burnell

4   Esquiers and Thomas Fanshawe gent[leman] by vertue of the quenes

5   Ma[jest]t[ies] Co[m]mission hereunto annexed sayeth upon his othe that

6   he hath receyved sithens[1] Easter last of dyvers p[er]sons

7   hereafter named prested[2] by hym by vertue of the quenes ma[jest]t[ies]

8   Co[m]mission made to S[i]r Richarde Leigh Knight to cary tymber

9   from the outwood[es] of Welbeck to Stockwith toward[es] the

10   cariage of suche lodes of tymber as he charged theyme ^to carye^ thither

11   dyvers so[m]mes of money folowinge

[1] *Since*

[2] *Payment advanced*

e.

1   Item pr[e]sentat[um] fuit etc in his Anglicanis verbis sequentib[us] (vi[delice]t)[1] That the

2   Owners and Landholders of the grounde Leading from Gubblecott brooke

3   downe to Long Marston have not observed and p[er]formed the payne and

4   Order made att the last Co[u]rte Leete for scowringe the ditch there accordinge

5   to the said Order then made et ideo in m[isericord]ia etc − vs[2]

6   Item pr[e]sentat[um] etc That Francis Hill hath not made upp his wall

7   next the Twitchell betweene Thomas Mathewes and himselfe accordinge

8   to a form[er] Order ideo in m[isericord]ia - iiis vid

[1] *'It was also presented in these English words following, namely …'*

[2] *'and therefore in mercy − 5s'*

f.

1   Inpr[im]is one close called the vicarage

2   close <…> conteyning one Acre in

3   the possession of the Parson

4   It[e]m a garden [and] an orchird adioyning

5   unto the vicarage howse being aboute

6   a q[ua]rter[1] of an acre of land belonging

7   unto the vicar

[1] *No mark of abbreviation*

g.

    Daye of Maye Anno 1573 and 15th yere

    of the R[eign] of Quene Elizabethe

1   John Dyer of Fratinge in the countie of Essex yoman beinge of hole minde and perfecte remembraunce

2   made his laste will and testamente in manner and fourme folowinge. Firste prepareinge
     him selfe to almightie god

3   Did will his boddye to be buried in the parrisshe churche of Fratinge. Item I give unto my
     4 childrenne that ys

4   John George Elizabethe and Anne to ev[er]ye of them £10 to be paide by my exec[utrix]
     when they shall attaine to the aige of

5   21 yeares. Item I give unto the childe that my wife is nowe w[i]t[h]all £10 to be paide at
     the like aige of 21 yeares [and]

6   yf yt fortune my saide childrenne or anye of them to dye before the said aige of 21 yeares.
     Then I will my exec[utrix]

7   to have theire p[ar]te ot p[ar]t[es] all the reste of my gooddes cattall[es] moveables
     specialties londs or leases whatsoev[er] I give unto

8   Anne my wife whome I make and ordaine my soale execut[rix] to see this my will
     performed…

EXERCISE 4.1

a.

Et q[uo]d Thomas Watt[es] unus tenenciu[m] d[omi]ni, de novo erexit duas cruces in
co[mmun]ia de Wymbildon, p[er] q[uo]d tenent[es] Abb[at]is Westm[onasterii] et tenent[es]
alio[rum] d[omi]no[rum], in Wannysworth, clamant injuste h[ab]er[e] co[mmun]iam
inf[r]a limites antiquas co[mmunion]is hui[us] d[oman]nii; in p[re]judiciu[m] d[omi]ni et
tenen[cium]: I[de]o prec[eptum] est bedell[o], q[uo]d scir[i] fac[iat] eid[e]m Thome, q[uo]d
sit ad p[ro]x[imam] cur[iam], ad respond[um] d[omi]no, de p[re]miss[is] et q[uo]d insup[er]
remover[i] fac[iat] cruc[es] p[re]dict[as], sub pe[n]a for[isfacti] ten[ementorum] et terr[arum]
suo[rum], que tenet de d[omi]no, s[e]c[un]d[u]m consuetud[inem] man[er]ii etc.

Translation:

And that Thomas Wattes, one of the tenants of the lord, erected anew two crosses on Wimbledon common, whereby
the tenants of the Abbot of Westminster and the tenants of other lords in Wandsworth claim unjustly to have
common within the ancient limits of the common of this demesne; to the prejudice of the lord and tenants. Therefore
the beadle is ordered to make it be known to the same Thomas that he should be at the next court to answer to the
lord concerning the premises, and that moreover he should cause the aforesaid crosses to be removed, under penalty of
forfeiting his tenements and lands, which he holds of the lord according to the custom of the manor etc.

b.

Wymbildon. Curia general[is] ejusd[e]m loci, tent[a] apud Putneth, die Lune p[ro]x[imo]
ante fest[um] app[osto]lo[rum] Simonis [et] Jude I Henry VII

Homagiu[m]. Comp[er]t[um] est p[er] inquis[icionem] homagii v[idelicet] p[er]
sacr[amentu]m Thome Pentecost (et septem al[iorum])
Et p[re]sent[ant] q[uo]d Joh[anne]es ^viijᵈ^ Bonar, vend[idit] bosc[am] ext[r]aniis, in
co[mmun]ia de Wymbildon' cont[r]a cons[uetudinem]; i[de]o in m[isericord]ia.
Et q[uo]d Ric[ard]us ^viᵈ^ Bonham occup[at] co[mmun]iam de Wymbildon, ubi null[am]
co[mmun]iam haberet: i[de]o ip[s]e in m[isericord]ia
M[isericord]ia iiˢ iiijᵈ

Translation:

Wimbledon. General court of the same place, held at Putney, on Monday next before the feast of the apostles Simon and Jude, I Henry VII.[1]

The Homage. It was found by inquiry of the homage, namely by the oath of Thomas Pentecost (and of seven others) And they present that John ^8d^ Bonar sold wood to strangers on Wimbledon common against the custom; therefore he is in mercy. And that Richard ^6d^ Bonham occupies Wimbledon common where he should not have common: therefore he is in mercy.
Amercement 2s 4d.

[1] *Monday, 24 October 1485. Table 4/I of Cheney's Handbook of Dates shows that the feast day of Simon and Jude is 28 October and is not a moveable feast; Table 2/II gives the regnal year of I Henry VII as 22 August 1485–21 August 1486 and refers the reader to Table 8,13 for the year 1485; 28 October, the feast day of Saints Simon and Jude, was a Friday that year, so the Monday before was 24 October*

EXERCISE 4.2

a.

1   Willm[us] Gardnor[1] sepult[us] fuit ultimo die mensis aprilis
2   in annis sup[er] script[is]
3   Thomas Sergent sepult[us] fuit 12° die mensis maii in
4   annis sup[er] script[is]

[1] *The entries were indexed online as Willing Garduno and Thomas Morgart*

Translation:

William Gardnor was buried on the last day of the month of April in the above-written years[2] *Thomas Sergent was buried on the twelfth day of the month of May in the above-written years.*

[2] *The 'above-written years' refer to the calendar year 1587 and Elizabeth I's regnal year 29*

b.

1   Mar[tius] 5 Joh[ann]es filius Joh[ann]is Tatam de Mapl'
2   Mar[tius] 16 Will[el]m[us] filius Rogeri Ballidon
3   Mar[tius] 16 Margretta filia [Christ]oferi Palmer[1]
4   Mar[tius] 17 Anna filia Will[el]mi Houlden Mapl'

[1] *Christopher Palmer was indexed online as Xpoferi Palmer*

Translation:

March 5 John son of John Tatam of Mapleton
March 16 William son of Roger Ballidon
March 16 Margaret daughter of Christopher Palmer
March 17 Ann daughter of William Houlden [of] Mapleton

c.

1   primo die baptizatus fuit puer
2   no[min]e Jacobus[1]
3   xxii° die Januarij baptizata fuit
4   Johan[na] Hitching[es] filia Thome
5   Hitching[es]
6   A[n]no d[omi]ni 1576

[1] *Unsurprisingly, given the handwriting, every entry on every page of the Latin part of this register was mistranscribed in the online index. The child baptised on the first day was indexed as Noe Jacobus*

Translation:

> *on the first day a boy named James was baptised*
> *on the 22nd day of January Joan Hitchinges daughter of Thomas Hitchinges was baptised*
> *in the year of the lord 1576*

EXERCISE 4.3

1	Freeman Page	William Fox
2	John Prat	William Nicholl[es]
3	John Dorchester	of Eastend
4	Anthony Webster	Robert Osborne
5	William Nicholls	Thomas Lyther
6	of Northend	John Cock[es]
7	Allen Knott	Thomas Sanders
8	John Walebanke	William Wetherly
9	William Marshe	Richard Rolffe
10	Thomas Nicholl	Francis Raven

EXERCISE 4.4

a.

1   Pr[e]ceptu[m] est Johanni May gen[er]oso facere sepes suas
2   bene et sufficienter, v[er]sus borealem p[ar]tem de le
3   wyndmyll hill aut aliter pati oves pascere quiet[e]
4   ut antea solent sub pena xs

Translation:

John May gentleman is ordered to make his fences well and adequately on the north side of Windmill Hill, or otherwise allow sheep to pasture peacefully as they were accustomed to do formerly under penalty of 10s.

b.

1   Item pr[e]sentant q[uo]d Humfridus Norris de Totteridge et Allanus Snowe de
2   eadem foderunt sabulu[m] in vasto d[omi]ni huius Man[er]ii et ill[ud] abcariaverunt extra p[ar]ochiam

3   de Finchley usq[ue] Totteridge pred[ictam] Ideo uterqu[e] eor[um] in m[isericord]ia – x[ls]
4   Ac etiam quod Georgius Hickes de p[ar]ochia de fryen sup[er]on[er]avit Co[mmun]em de Finchley
5   cu[m] ovib[us] Ideo ip[s]e in m[isericord]ia - v[li]
6   Ad hanc Cur[iam] venit Rob[er]tus Rolffe ^et recog[novit] se tenere^ de d[omi]nis un[um] ten[emen]tu[m] apud finem vie in Finchley
7   et tres Cl[ausur]as ib[ide]m nup[er] p[at]ris d[ic]ti Rob[er]ti et fecit inde fid[elitatem]

Translation:

They also present that Humphrey Norris of Totteridge and Allan Snowe of the same dug gravel in the waste of the lord of this manor and carried it out of the parish of Finchley to the aforesaid Totteridge. Therefore both of them are in mercy – £10. And also that George Hickes of the parish of Friern overloaded the common of Finchley with sheep. Therefore he is in mercy – £5. To this court came Robert Rolffe and acknowledged that he holds from the lords one tenement at the end of the road in Finchley and three closes there formerly of the father of the said Robert, and he made fealty in respect thereof.

EXERCISE 4.5

1   Ad hanc Cur[iam] p[re]sentatu[m] est per homagiu[m] quod Richardus Larchin de Istleworth
2   Fysherman iacens in extremis sursu[m] Reddidit in manus d[omi]ni manerii per manus et
3   acceptacionem Joh[ann]is Butler et Thome Prymer duoru[m] Custumar[iorum] tenentiu[m]
4   huius manerii duo Cottagia cum p[er]tinenciis in Istleworthe quoru[m] unu[m] modo est
5   in occupacione p[re]dicte[1] Thome Prymer et alteru[m] nup[er] fuit in occupacione
6   vidue Lewes et Tres acras terr[e] Custumar[ie], quaru[m] due acre et dimid[ia]
7   iacent in stratfurlong, et alia dimid[ia] acra iacet in Mogdon in p[ar]ochia
8   de Istleworthe. Ad opus et usum Edmundi Larchin <...> filii p[re]dicti Richardi
9   et hered[um] suoru[m] imp[er]petuu[m] Cui dominus per Senescall[um] suu[m] Concessit inde
10   seisinam habend[a] et tenend[a] p[re]fato Edmundo Larchin et heredibus suis ad
11   voluntatem d[omi]ni secund[um] Consuetud[inem] manerii reddend[o] inde Domino de   Reddit[u] per
12   annu[m] ii[s] iij[d] et faciend[o] omnia alia Consuetud[ines] et servicia inde prius debita
13   et de iure Consueta Dat D[omi]no de fine et herriett[o] p[ro] duobus Cottagiis ii[s]
14   et de fine terr[e] xij[d] fecit fidelitatem et admissus est inde Tenens.

[1] *This should be 'predicti'*

Translation:

At this court it was presented by the homage that Richard Larchin of Isleworth, fisherman, lying at the point of death, surrendered into the hands of the lord of the manor by the hands and acceptance of John Butler and Thomas Prymer, two customary tenants of this manor, two cottages with appurtenances in Isleworth, of which one is now in the occupation of the aforesaid Thomas Prymer, and the other was lately in the occupation of the widow Lewes, and three acres of customary land, of which two and a half acres lie in Stratfurlong, and the other half acre lies in Mogdon in the the parish of Isleworth. To the benefit and use of Edmund Larchin, son of the aforesaid Richard, and his heirs for ever. To whom the lord by his steward granted seisin therein, to have and to hold to the aforesaid Edmund Larchin and his heirs, at the will of the lord according to the custom of the manor, by rendering in respect thereof to the Lord rent of 2s 3d a year, and by undertaking all customs and services therein formerly owed and by right accustomed. He gives to the lord as fine and heriot for the two cottages 2s and as fine of land 12d. He did fealty and was therein admitted tenant.

EXERCISE 4.6

1   Joh[ann]es Bragge gen[erosus] Recogn[ovit][1] tenere per copiam
2   Rot[u]lo[rum] Cur[ie] unu[m] mesuagi[um] et xxiiii[or] acr[as] terre
3   p[er] estim[acionem] voc[ata] ^upper^ Typlond[es] <...> iacen[tes] iuxta
4   terr[as] man[er]ii de Holton' v[er]s[us] boriam [et] terr[as]
5   man[er]ii de Spandbyes in Stratford v[er]s[us]
6   orien[tem] et occiden[tem] Et Redd[it] p[er] Ann[um] –
7   p[er]quisit[um] de Will[elmo] Bragge de Bulmer
8   circa viginti Annos elapsos

[1] *'se' missing*

Translation:

John Bragge gentleman acknowledged that he holds by copy of the court rolls one messuage and by estimation 24 acres of land called 'Upper Typlondes' lying next to the lands of the manor of Holton towards the north and the lands of the manor of Spanbies in Stratford towards the east and west. And he pays each year – . Acquisition of William Bragge of Bulmer around twenty years past.

EXERCISE 4.7

a.
1   ... Qui dicunt super Sacr[ament]um suum quod pred[ictus] Johannes
2   Smith per spatium duodecem dierum ante Capc[i]onem huius Inquisic[i]o[n]is languebat infra gaola[m]
3   pred[i]c[t]am de quadam infirmitate vocat[a] 'a pyninge sicknes' Et de eadem infirmitate decimo nono
4   die eiusdem mensis Maii anno regni d[i]c[t]e D[omi]ne Regine tricesimo secundo suprad[i]c[t]o idem Johannes
5   Smith in quodam loco infra eandem Goalam vocat[o] the Middle Warde ex visitac[i]one divina obiit
6   Et sic idem Johannes Smith ad mortem suam devenit, et non al[ite]r neq[ue] aliquo alio modo. In
7   cuius rei testimonium etc.

Translation:

Who say upon their oath that the aforesaid John Smith for the space of twelve days before the taking of this inquest lay ill within the aforesaid gaol from a certain sickness called 'a pining sickness'. And from the same sickness on the nineteenth day of the same month of May in the above-mentioned thirty-second year of the reign

of the said Lady Queen [19 May 1590] the same John Smith in a certain place within the same gaol called the
Middle Ward died from divine visitation. And thus the same John Smith came to his death, and not otherwise
nor in any other way. In witness of which etc.

b.

1   Ad hanc Curia[m] pr[e]sentatu[m] fuit p[er] homagiu[m] q[uo]d Will[el]mus Collins de
2   Twickenham Sursu[m] reddidit in manus domini p[er] manus et acceptac[i]onem
3   [Christ]opheri Udall et Joh[ann]is Wixe duorum Custumarioru[m] tenentiu[m]
4   mencrii Una[m] dimid[iam] acra[m] terre errabilis iacen[tem] in australi Campo
5   de Twickenham in shotta[1] vocata laneum inter terr[am] magistre
6   Gylman ex p[ar]te orientali et terr[am] Roberti Baker ex p[ar]te occidental[i]
7   Ad opus et usum ^dicti^ Roberti Baker et Alicie uxoris eius et hered[um]
8   suor[um] imp[er]petuu[m] Cui dominus p[er] Senescalum Concessit inde
9   sei[sin]am Habend[am] et tenend[am] pr[e]fato Roberto Baker et ^Alicie uxori eius^ hered[ibus] suis
10 imp[er]petuu[m] Secund[um] Consuetud[inem] manerii reddend[o] et faciend[o] inde
11 domino op[er]a Consuetud[ines] et servit[ia] inde prius debit[a] et de iure
12 Consuet[a] <fecit> ^fecerunt^ fidelitatem et admiss<us>i <est> sunt inde tenentes

[1] *Shot: part of an open field with all the strips going the same way and a headland at each end*

Translation:

It was presented at this court by the homage that William Collins of Twickenham surrendered into the hands
of the lord by the hands and acceptance of Christopher Udall and John Wixe, two of the customary tenants
of the manor, one half acre of arable land lying in the southern field of Twickenham in a shot called 'laneum'
between the land of master Gylman on the eastern side and the land of Robert Baker on the western side, to the
benefit and use of the said Robert Baker and his wife and their heirs for ever. To whom the lord by his steward
granted seisin therein to have and to hold to the aforesaid Robert Baker and Alice his wife and their heirs for
ever according to the custom of the manor, rendering and making in respect thereof to the lord works customary
services and services formerly owed and by right accustomed. They did fealty and were admitted tenants therein.

c.

1   Idem Joh[ann]es Bragge tenet lib[ere] p[er] Cartam
2   un[um] Ten[emen]tum vocat[um] Thornes [et] vii acras
3   terre adiacen[tis] iacen[tes] in Stratford iuxta
4   terr[as] man[er]ii de Spandbyes v[er]s[us] orien[tem]
5   et boriam [et] terr[as] Jacobi Bragge v[er]s[us]
6   Austrum, et terr[as] Custom[ar]ias p[re]di[ctas] Joh[ann]is
7   Bragg sup[ra] menc[i]onat[i] v[er]s[us] occident[em]
8   p[er] Redd[itum] – x^s
9   nup[er] <...> Rob[er]t[i] Bragge et antea Joh[ann]is Bragge

Translation

The same John Bragge holds freely by deed one tenement called 'Thornes' and 7 acres of adjacent land lying in Stratford next to the lands of the manor of Spanbies towards the east and north, and the lands of James Bragge towards the south, and the aforesaid customary lands of the above-mentioned John Bragge towards the west, by rent – 10s. Late of Robert Bragge and formerly of John Bragge.

d.

1   Qui dicunt super Sacr[ament]um suu[m] quod vicesimo primo die Julij anno

2   regni d[i]c[t]e D[omi]ne n[ost]re Elizabethe nunc Regine Anglie etc Tricesimo secundo suprad[i]c[t]o circa horam

3   prima[m] in aurora eiusdem diei pr[e]fat[us] Nich[ola]us Sherrott et quidam Josephus Cater waterman

4   insimul v[e]niebant subter pontem Civitatis London' vocat[um] London Bridge sup[er] fluviu[m] thamesis

5   in quadam cymba vocata a Whirrey existen[ti] onerat[a] cum quadam p[ar]cella casei ubi tunc et ib[ide]m ita

6   accidit quod eadem cymba per vigorem et violentia[m] fluvii et aquar[um] a dict[o] ponte tunc et ibidem

7   Confluentiu[m] violenter subacta fuit sup[er] quendam lintrem vocat[um] a lighter Cuiusdam hominis

8   ignot[i] valor[is] quadraginta sollidorum iacente[m] et existent[em] ad rodam anglice at roade in dicto

9   fluvio Thamesis prope quendam locum vocatu[m] Colde Harbo[u]r in p[ar]ochia Omniu[m] Sanctorum

10   magnoru[m] in warda Pontis infra London' Qui quidem Linter Anglice Barge eandem cymba[m]

11   adeo vehementer tunc et ib[ide]m quassabat et confligebat Ita ut eadem cymba sup[er] inde valde

12   fracta et lacerat[a] fuit Anglice was rent and splitt, rac[i]one Cuius cymba pr[e]d[icta] una cum eodem

13   Nicholao in fluviu[m] pr[e]d[ictum] imediate evertebat, et sic idem Nich[ola]us tunc et ib[ide]m submersus et

14   suffocat[us] fuit Et in eodem fluvio tunc et ib[ide]m instanter obiit. Et sic Juratores pr[e] d[icti] sup[er]

15   Sacr[ament]um suu[m] predict[um] dicunt quod pred[i]c[t]us Nich[ola]us Sherrott per infortuniu[m] et Contra

16   voluntatem suam modo et forma pr[e]d[ictis] ad mortem suam devenit et non aliter neq[ue] aliquo

17   alio modo, Et quod eadem cymba est valoris quinq[ue] sollidor[um] et remanet in Custodia pr[e]d[icti]

18   Josephi Cater ad opus et usum d[i]c[t]e D[omi]ne Regine. In cuius rei Testimoniu[m] etc

Translation:

Who say upon their oath that on the twenty-first day of July in the abovesaid thirty-second year of the reign of our said Lady Elizabeth now queen of England etc [21 July 1590] around the first hour at daybreak of the same day, the aforesaid Nicholas Sherrott and a certain Joseph Cater waterman together came below the bridge of the City of London called London Bridge upon the river Thames in a certain small boat called a 'whirrey' being loaded with a certain parcel of cheese when then and there it happened that the same whirrey was driven down violently by the strength and violence of the river and waters then and there flowing from the said bridge, upon a certain small boat called a 'lighter' worth 40s belonging to a certain unknown man, lying and being at road (in English 'at roade') in the said river Thames near a certain place called Cold Harbour in the parish of All Hallows the Great in the ward of Bridge Within London. Which small boat, in English a 'barge', violently then and there to such an extent battered and struck the same whirrey on account of which it was greatly broken and shattered, in English 'was rent and splitt', by reason of which the aforesaid whirrey along with the same Nicholas was immediately overturned into the river, and thus the same Nicholas then and there was submerged and suffocated. And in the same river then and there instantly he died. And thus the aforesaid jurors say upon their oath that the aforesaid Nicholas Sherrott through misfortune and against his will in the manner and form aforesaid came by his death and not otherwise nor in any other way. And that the aforesaid whirrey is of the value of 5s. and remains in the custody of the aforesaid Joseph Cater to the benefit and use of the said Lady Queen.

EXERCISE 5.1

1   In the name of god Amen the second day of the moneth[1] of Jule the yere of our lord

2   god 1463 and the yere of the Reigne of Kyng Edward the 4th the 3d I

3   John Frost citezein and mercer of London hoole in mynde and helth of body thus ordeygne

4   and make this my p[re]sent testament and my last Will Beseching almyghty god to be

5   goode guyde by the meritt[es] of all the saintez of heven First I biqueth my soule to all

6   myghty god my maker and my Redemer unto our lady and all the saintez of heven

7   And my body to be buryed in the Chircheyerd of our lady in Aldermanbury in the

8   brode Aley by fore the porche of the same chirch And I biqueth to the high Auter

9   for tithes and offeringes slouched and forgetyn in tyme passed and to be Remembred

10   of my curate and prayed for 20s It[e]m to the chirch werkys and the stypell

11   esp[esc]ialy 26s 8d It[e]m to yche[2] prest of the chirche ev[er]y quarter of the yer[e]

12   folowyng 4d beside my obite[3] for to Remembr[e] my poure soule in their devocions

13   4 tymes in the yer[e] It[e]m to be geven in almes to the moost needy housholders in …

[1] *There are several marks of abbreviation in this and the following letter, which are probably otiose and are not noted here*

[2] *Each*

[3] *An 'obit' was a service held for the soul of the deceased on the anniversary of their death*

EXERCISE 5.2

1   My Worschipfull Cosyn I Recomaund me toyow pleasith yow I have spoken with harper

2   like as ye willid me and as for yo[u]r mat[ter] he seith hit is ferre in the law [and] wolbe sued to the

3   utterist acordy[n]g to yo[u]r title Wherfor he desired that my Cosyn hampden [and] harry doget may

4   have knowlage that they do no thy[n]g co[n]trarie to your title. I have taken hanygton 7

5   nobils[1] [and] to S[i]r Ric[hard] harcourt 20 ma[r]cs[2] the seid S[i]r Ric[hard] desyri[n]g
    <...> to know the weys [and] days
6   how he shalbe content of his £100 beyng verray hasty theraft I seid tohym wha[n] he
7   [and] ye mete ye wold appoynt w[i]t[h] hym that shold please hym. sith[3] I cam to towne
    I have
8   be bothe at Phisikke [and] surgery I thank god of amendeme[n]t my purs therby gretly
9   appeyrid[4] I p[r]ay god be with yow [and] spede yow in all your doyng[es] at lundon the
10 saturday aftir seynt martyn day
    Thomas Ramsey

[1] *A noble was a gold coin worth 6s 8d*
[2] *A mark was a unit of currency worth two-thirds of a pound sterling, 13s 4d*
[3] *Since*
[4] *Appaired: impaired*

EXERCISE 5.3

a.
1   M[emoran]d[um] theise be the names underwretyn that held ther Ten[emen]t[es]
    w[i]t[h]in the Town of Bury Seynt Edmu[n]de long
2   tyme after [and] byfore the 21[th] yer of the Reigne of Kyng Edward the furst the whiche
    paid certeyn
3   Rent unto the monastery ther whiche Rent was [and] ys dysinable unto the same
    mon[astery] and the
4   veray Ten[emen]t[es] the self were than [and] yet be Taxable and owe to pay Taxe to the
    Kyng
5   whan yt ys callyd upon etc

b.
1   Extenta manerii de Claverleg' f[ac]ta p[er] hos subscriptos Thom[am] de Upton[1]
    Walt[eru]m Halet Thom[am] Bot[er]el
2   Rob[ertu]m de la Bolde Ph[ilippu]m de Gyrros Hugo[ne]m de Baskervill Hug[onem] de
    Halicot Aung[er]um de
3   Oudon Hug[onem] de Binsedeleg' Warn[eru]m de Beyssin Rog[eru]m de Foxcot
    Rad[ulphu]m Sprengehose Jur[atores] de Stottesdon Rob[ertu]m de Bispeston'
    Ivone[m] de Brotton' Rog[eru]m Bag Rad[ulphu]m de Staunton Henr[icum]
4   de Bispeston Will[elmu]m Champeneys Ad[a]m Pollard Joh[anne]m de Ryton Rog[eru]
    m de Halehton Joh[ann]em de
5   Grenhull Nich[olau]m de Rugge [et] Ric[ardu]m de Wrottesleg' Jur[atores] de
    Brenestre qui dicunt sup[er] sacr[amentu]m
6   suu[m] q[uo]d sunt in eod[e]m man[er]io Tres virgate t[er]re in d[o]m[ini]co q[u]arum
    quelibet valet p[er] annu[m] cu[m] pastura
7   octo solid[os]   S[um]ma xxiiii[or] sol[idi]

[1] *Possibly otiose marks of abbreviation at the ends of place names are not recorded here*

Translation:

Extent of the manor of Claverley made by these underwritten [there follows a list of jurors] who say upon their oath that in the same manor there are three virgates of land in the demesne each worth 8s a year with pasture.
Sum 24 shillings.

EXERCISE 5.4

a.

1   Hec est finalis concordia f[a]c[t]a in Cur[ia] d[omi]ni Regis apud Westm[onasterium] in Crastino purificat[i]o[n]is

2   b[eat]e Marie anno Regnor[um] Henrici Regis Angl[ie] [et] Franc[ie] septimi a conquestu decimo nono

3   coram Thoma Frowyk Will[elm]o Danvers Joh[ann]e Vavasour [et] Joh[ann]e Fyssher Justic[iariis] [et] aliis d[omi]ni

4   Regis fidelib[us] tunc ibi p[re]sentib[us] Int[er] Edmundu[m] Hyll Edwardu[m] Hyll Ric[ardu]m Martyn [et]

5   Joha[nne]m Redforde quer[entes] et Will[elmu]m Wynchester deforc[iantem] de uno mesuagio triginta acris t[er]re

6   decem acris prati [et] trib[us] acris bosci cu[m] p[er]tin[enciis] in Dytton sup[er] Thamis' [et] Emworth unde

7   pl[aci]t[um] convenc[i]o[n]is sum[monitum] fuit int[er] eos in eadem Cur[ia] Scil[ice]t …

Translation:

This is the final concord made in the Court of the Lord King at Westminster on the morrow of the Purification of the Blessed Mary in the nineteenth years of the reigns of King Henry the Seventh of England and France from the Conquest [3 February 1504] before Thomas Frowyk, William Danvers, John Vavasour and John Fyssher justices and other faithful of the Lord King then there present between Edmund Hyll, Edward Hyll, Richard Martyn and John Redforde plaintiffs and William Wynchester deforciant concerning one messuage, thirty acres of land, ten acres of meadow and three acres of wood with appurtenances in Ditton upon Thames and Emworth, in respect whereof a plea of convenant was summoned between them in the same court, namely …

b.

Margin: Man[er]iu[m] de Ham' iuxta Kyngeston'

1   Cur[ia] Prima Baron[is] excellentissime d[omi]ne marie prime dei gra[tia] Angl[ie]

2   Franc[ie] et Hib[er]n[ie] Regine fidei defensoris et in t[er]ra eccl[es]ie Anglicane

3   et Hib[er]nice sup[re]mi Capitis ib[ide]m tent[a] sexto die Octobr[is] Anno

4   regni d[i]c[t]e d[omi]ne Primo

Translation:

Manor of Ham next Kingston

First court baron of the most excellent lady, Mary the first, by grace of God queen of England, France and Ireland, defender of the faith, and supreme head on earth of the English and Irish church, held there on the sixth day of October in the first year of the reign of the said lady [6 October 1553]

1   Qui dicunt sup[er] sacr[a]m[entum] suu[m] q[uo]d Swithin[us] Welles Will[elmu]s
     Roydon hered[es] Laurencii

2   Thorley Thomas Morer Joh[ann]es Pyke de London' Rob[er]tus Smyth hered[es]
     Swithin[i] Skerne

3   Humfr[id]us Ley Thomas Redknappe in iure ux[or]is sue

Translation:

Who say upon their oath that Swithin Welles, William Roydon, the heirs of Laurence Thorley, Thomas Morer, John Pyke of London, Robert Smyth, the heirs of Swithin Skerne, Humphrey Ley, Thomas Redknappe by right of his wife …

c.

1   Memorand[um] Q[uo]d Will[elm]us Bellamy Ar[miger] Coron[arius] [et] Attorn[atus]
     D[omi]ni Regis in Cur[ia] ip[s]ius Regis coram ip[s]o Rege

2   qui p[ro] eod[e]m D[omi]no Rege in hac p[ar]te sequitur in p[ro]pr[ia] p[er]son[a] sua
     ven[it] hic in Cur[iam] d[i]c[t]i D[omi]ni Regis coram ip[s]o

3   Rege apud Westm[onasterium] die m[er]cur[ii] p[roximo] p[os]t Quinden[am] Pasche
     isto eod[e]m Termi[n]o [et] p[ro] eod[e]m

4   D[omi]no Rege ex relac[i]on[e] Ric[ard]i Score de Barnestaple in Com[itatu] Devon[ie]
     Ar[migeri] s[e]c[un]d[u]m form[am] Statut[i]

5   in hoc casu edit[i] [et] p[ro]vis[i] dat Cur[iam] hic Intelligi [et] Informari q[uo]d Burgus
     de Lostwithiel in Com[itatu] Cornub[ie]

6   est antiquus Burgus q[uo]dq[ue] maior [et] Burgenses eiusd[e]m Burgi sunt [et] p[er]
     viginti Annos iam ult[imos]

7   elaps[os] et diu antea fuer[unt] un[um] Corpus Corporatu[m] et politicu[m] in re f[a]c[t]o
     [et] no[m]i[n]e p[er] no[m]en maior[is] et Burgensiu[m] Burgi de

8   Lostwithiel in Com[itatu] Cornub[ie] …

Translation:

Let it be remembered that William Bellamy esquire, coroner and attorney of the lord King, in the court of the King himself, before the King himself, who in this behalf prosecutes in his own person for the same lord King, comes here into the court of the said lord King before the King himself at Westminster on Wednesday next after the quinzaine of Easter in this same term, and for the same lord King, upon information of Richard Score, esquire, of Barnstaple in the county of Devonshire, according to the form of the statute published and provided in this case, gives the court here to understand and be informed that the borough of Lostwithiel in the county of Cornwall is an ancient borough and that the mayor and burgesses of the same borough are and for twenty years now last past and for a long time before were one body corporate and politic in deed, fact and name, by the name of the mayor and burgesses of the borough of Lostwithiel in the county of Cornwall.

d.

1   Cur[ia] D[omi]ne Regine Honoris sui p[re]d[icti] a trib[us] septiman[is] in tres
     Septiman[as] s[e]c[un]d[u]m

2   Consuetud[inem] eiusd[e]m honor[is] tent[a] apud le Whitehart in Yeldham magn[a] infra

3   honor[em] ill[um] Die Jovis decimo Die Januarii Anno regni D[omi]ne Anne magne

4   Britanie Franc[ie] [et] Hib[er]nie Regine Fidei Defensor[is] etc decimo coram
     Nathanael[i]

5   Plinne gen[eroso] Joh[ann]is Rotheram Ar[migeri] Capitalis Sene[sca]lli ib[ide]m
     l[eg]ittime constitut[o]
6   subseneschallo
7   Joh[ann]es Dawson [et] Jacobu[s] Mosse Attach[iati] agard[o] in p[ro]x[ima] Cur[ia]
8   Id[e]m [et] Georgiu[s] Mosse Attach[iati] Agard[o]

Translation:

Court of the aforesaid honour of the lady queen [held] every three weeks according to the custom of the same
honour, held at the White Hart in Great Yeldham within that honour, on Thursday the tenth of January in the
tenth year of the reign of the lady Anne, queen of Great Britain, France and Ireland, defender of the faith etc
[10 January 1712] before Nathaniel Plinne, gentleman, lawfully appointed sub-steward of John Rotheram,
esquire, chief steward there.
John Dawson [and] James Mosse Attached for decision at the next court.
The same and George Mosse Attached for decision.

EXERCISE 5.5

1   Memorand[um] q[uo]d Ph[ilipp]us Yorke mil[es] Attorn[atus] D[omi]ni Regis nunc
     Gen[er]al[is] qui p[ro] eod[e]m D[omi]no Rege
2   in hac parte sequitur in p[ro]pr[ia] p[er]sona sua venit hic in Cur[ia] d[i]c[t]i D[omi]ni
     Regis coram ip[s]o Rege
3   apud Westm[onasterium] die mercur[ii] p[ro]x[imo] post tres Septi[m]an[as] s[an]c[t]e
     Trin[itatis] isto eod[e]m T[er]mi[n]o Et p[ro] eod[e]m D[omi]no
4   Rege dat Cur[iam] hic intelligi et informari Q[uo]d Joh[ann]es Purser de London'
     Typographus existens
5   homo malitiosus seditiosus et maledispositus ac p[er]petuus et assiduus Publicator et
6   Venditor f[a]l[s]or[um] seditiosor[um] et scandalosor[um] libellor[um] ac d[i]c[t]o
     D[omi]no Regi nunc ac ad[mini]strac[i]on[i]
7   sue Gub[er]nac[i]on[is] hui[us] r[eg]ni maleaffect[or] ac Fautor p[er]sone in vita Jacobi
     s[e]c[un]di nup[er] Regis
8   Angl[ie] etc p[re]ten[denti]s esse principis Wallie [et] post d[i]c[t]i nup[er] Regis
     decessu[m] p[re]tenden[tis] esse et suscipien[tis]
9   sup[er] se Stilum [et] Tit[u]l[u]m Regis Angl[ie] p[er] no[m]en Jacobi t[er]tii …

Translation:

Let it be remembered that Philip Yorke knight, attorney general of our present lord King, who in this behalf
prosecutes in his own person for the same lord King, comes here to the court of the said lord King before the
King himself at Westminster on Wednesday next after three weeks from Holy Trinity in this same term, and
for the same lord King gives the court here to understand and be informed that John Purser, printer of London,
being a wicked, seditious and ill-disposed man, and a long-standing and assiduous publisher and seller of
false, seditious and scandalous libels, malefactor to the said present lord King and to the administration of
his government of this realm, adherent of the person pretending in the life of James the Second late king of
England etc to be the prince of Wales and after the death of the said king pretending to be and taking the
style and title upon himself of King of England in the name of James the Third [did cause to be printed
and published …]

EXERCISE 5.6

a.

1   Whereas Alyce Higham Wydowe late wyffe of Thomas Higham of Shewdye Camps in the Countie

2   of Cambridge deceased and Robert Higham the yonger sonne of the sayd Thomas have exhibyted

3   theyr bill of Complaynt into this honorable Courte of Chauncery agaynst George Higham Deff[endant]

4   declaryng by the same that where the said Thomas in his lyffe tyme was lawfully seased in his

5   demeane as of Fee of and in a house called mascall[es] with the landes therunto belongyng sett

6   lyinge and beynge in the Towne [and] feldes of Shewdye Camps aforesaid and the p[ro]ffyttes therof

7   durynge all his lyfe lawfully toke [and] p[er]ceyved to his owne use and comodyte without any lett

b.

1   Rex Escaetori suo in Com[itatu] Essex Sal[u]t[e]m Cum p[er] quandam Inquisic[i]o[n]em

2   coram Edwardo D[omi]no Dennye Joh[ann]e Doddridge Armig[er]o nup[er] solicitatore

3   n[ost]ro gen[er]al[i] Ric[ard]o Francke Ar[migero] Joh[ann]e Edward[es] Armig[er]o nup[er] Escaetore

4   n[ost]ro Com[itatus] p[re]dict[i] [et] Will[elm]o Courtman gen[eroso] Feodario n[ost]ro eiusdem Com[itatus] …

Translation:

The King [gives] greeting to his eschaetor in the county of Essex. Since by a certain inquiry before Edward lord Denny, John Doddridge esquire late our solicitor general, Richard Francke esquire, John Edwards esquire late our escheator of the aforesaid county, and William Courtman gentleman feodary of the same county …

c.

1   Charles the Second by the grace of god king of England

2   Scotland France and Ireland defendor of the Faith etc

3   To our Treasurer Vicetreasurer Cheife Baron and the

4   rest of the Barons of our Court of Exchequer …

1   An Improvement of the wast land[es] and soyle of the Forrest

2   of Deane in the County of Gloucester was then made by the

3   then Surveyor Generall and other Com[m]issioners deputed for

4   that service by the Com[m]ission under the Great Seale of England

5   and an allottment of foure thousand acres thereof was

6   then alsoe made to the Freeholders claymeing Com[m]on in

7   the said Forrest and to the poore of the adiacent villages

8   in full satisfact[i]on of their pretended right of Com[m]on

d.

1   paid the Testators widow Nine months
2   of her Annuity due the twenty first of
3   January last
4   paid M[aste]r Garmson more pursuant to the
5   said Order for the Dividend on south sea
6   stock at Christmass One thousand seven
7   hundred and twenty five

EXERCISE 5.7

a.

1   Sciant p[re]sentes [et] futuri q[uo]d Ego Radulphus Parle de mangna Fransham concessi
     dedi et hac p[re]senti carta mea confirmavi Kate
2   rine filie Rog[er]i cl[er]ici de Coltune unam acram terre mee in villa de p[ar]va Fransham
     q[ue] iacet ap[u]d pot[er]iscroft scil[ice]t int[er] t[er]ram
3   Will[elm]i de Aula[1] v[er]sus aq[ui]lone[m] et t[er]ram Alex[andr]i Lest[r]ange
     v[er]s[us] austru[m] [et] habuttac[ulum] sup[er] pa[r]cum d[i]c[t]i Alex[andr]i vers[us]
     occidentem
4   [et] aliud cap[u]d s[upe]r[?] regalem viam vers[us] oriente[m] Tenenda[m] [et]
     Habend[am] d[i]c[t]e Kat[er]ine et heredibus suis v[e]l assignatis suis
5   v[e]l cuicu[m]q[ue] [et] q[u]a[n]docu[m]q[ue] p[re]d[i]c[t]am t[er]ram dare vendere
     legare v[e]l assignare voluerit tam in eg[ri]tudine q[u]am in sanitate
6   In feodo [et] he[re]ditate libere q[ui]ete bene [et] in pace Reddendo inde annuati[m]
     Thome de Esthen [et] heredibus suis …

[1] *At this date, surnames were often rendered into Latin. See The Record Interpreter for a list of Latin forms of
English surnames. If in doubt, leave the surname in its Latin form*

Translation:

*Let those present and future know that I Ralph Parle of Great Fransham have granted, given, and by this my
charter have confirmed to Catherine, daughter of Roger Clerk of Colton, one acre of my land in the town of
Little Fransham which lies at Potterscroft, namely between the land of William Hall towards the north, and
the land of Alexander Lestrange towards the south, and the dwelling place upon the park of the said Alexander
on the west and another headland upon [?] the king's highway towards the east, to have and hold to the same
Catherine and her heirs or assigns or to whomsoever and whensoever she might wish to give, sell, leave or assign
the aforesaid land, both in sickness and in health, in fee and inheritance, freely, quietly, rightly and in peace,
paying annually in respect thereof to Thomas de Esthen and his heirs …*

b.

1   Hec est finalis concordia f[a]c[t]a in Cur[ia] d[omi]ne Regine apud Westm[onasterium]
     in Crastino
2   S[anc]te Trinitatis Anno regno[rum] Elizabeth[e] dei gra[tia] Angl[ie] Franc[ie] [et]
     Hib[er]n[ie]
3   Regine fidei defensoris etc A conqu[estu] quarto coram Jacobo Dyer Humfr[id]o
4   Broun[1] Antonio Broun et Ric[ard]o Weston Justic[iariis] Et postea in Octabis S[anc]ti

5   Mich[ael]is Anno regno[rum] eiusd[e]m Regine Elizabeth[e] sup[ra]d[i]c[t]o ib[ide]m
      concessa

6   [et] recordata coram eisd[e]m Justic[iariis] [et] aliis d[omi]ne Regine fidelib[us] tunc

7   ibi p[re]sentib[us] Int[er] John[ann]em Holmden quer[entem] et Georgiu[m] Holmden
      [et]

8   Margaretam ux[or]em eius deforc[iantes] de quatuor acris pasture [et] duab[us] acris

9   bosci cum p[er]tin[enciis] in Tatsfeld unde pl[ac]it[u]m convenc[i]o[n]is sum[monitum]
      fuit int[er] eos in ead[e]m

10   Cur[ia] Scil[ice]t q[uo]d p[re]d[i]c[t]i Georgius et Margareta recogn[overunt]
      p[re]d[i]c[t]a ten[ementa] cum p[er]tin[enciis] esse

11   Ius ip[s]ius John[ann]is ut illa que id[e]m John[ann]es h[ab]et de dono p[re]d[i]c[t]o[rum]
      Georgii [et]

12   Margarete Et illa remiser[unt] et quietumclamav[erunt] de ipsis Georgio et Margareta
      [et]

13   hered[ibus] ip[s]ius Georgii p[re]d[i]c[t]o John[ann]i et hered[ibus] suis Imp[er]p[etuu]m

[1] *The surnames have marks of abbreviation that are probably otiose, and so are not recorded here*

Translation:

This is the final agreement made in the court of the lady queen at Westminster on the morrow of Holy Trinity in the fourth year of the reigns of Elizabeth after the conquest, by grace of God queen of England, France and Ireland, defender of the faith etc [25 May 1562], before James Dyer, Humphrey Broun, Anthony Broun and Richard Weston justices, and afterwards on the Octave of Saint Michael in the abovesaid year of the reigns of the same queen Elizabeth, there granted and recorded before the same justices and other faithful people of the lady then there present, between John Holmden, plaintiff, and George Holmden and Margaret his wife, defendants, concerning four acres of pasture and two acres of woodland with appurtenances in Tatsfield, whereupon a plea of covenant was summoned between them in the same court, to wit that the aforesaid George and Margaret have acknowledged the aforesaid tenements with appurtenances to be the right of John himself as those which the same John has by the gift of George and Margaret themselves. And those they have remised and quitclaimed from George and Margaret themselves and the heirs of George himself to the aforesaid John and his heirs for ever …

c.
1   Whereas in the cause dependinge in this Courte
2   by English bill betwixte John Winchecombe the elder and John
3   Kerry Esquires and John Winchecombe the younger gent[leman]
4   Complaynants and Henry Norton Walter Norton and Anthony
5   Bedingfeild Esquiers and Robert Morse gent[leman] defendants touchinge
6   severall bonds the one of two thowsand eight hundred pounds
7   the other of three hundred pounds entred into by the Complaynants

d.
1   itt was found that Sarah James late of Rockland
2   St Peter in the said County widow att Thassizes [and] gen[er]all Gaole
3   deliv[er]y held att Thetford then last past was attaynted of Petty Treason [and]
4   that att the tyme of her said Attaynder she was amongst other things

5 seized as of Fee [and] right of [and] in the advowson [and] right of p[ar]sonage of
6 the Rectorie [and] Church of Rockland St Peeter

e.
1 Tenant[es] att wyll
2 Inp[ri]mis Rychard dowson holdyth two oxgan[ge][1]
3 off arable land and payth therefore yerely
4 It[em] george hull one Cottage ^3s 4d^ and two oxgange off
5 lande ^26s 8d^
6 It[em] John Collyngson one Cottage ^6s 8d^ and one oxgan[ge] ^13s 4d^ off
7 land
8 It[em] John Cottom one cottage
9 It[em] Thomas Waferer one mease[2] ^6s 8d^ and 4 oxgan[ge] ^53s 4d^ off land
10 It[em] Thomas Marshall one Cottage
11 It[em] Nycolas Johnson one mease ^6s 8d^ and 4 oxg[ange] ^53s 4d^ off land

[1] *In the next line, the writer uses 'oxgange' as plural, so the word has been extended as this throughout*
[2] *Messuage*

f.
1 Rauff norres hold[es] a noxgange [and] hawf[1] of land
2 <...> [and] 6 ac[res] of rodde land[2] pays
3 yerly 14s 3 ½ d [and] hold[es] in wyntt[er] <...> 8 best 2 horsse[3]
4 thomas woddam hold[es] 2 p[ar]t[es] of a messe [and] 7 ac[res] of land
5 pays yerly 3s 6d he hold[es] in wyntt[er] 4 best[es] on horsse
6 Wyll[ia]m Bartelot hold[es] a messe hawf a noxgange of land
7 [and] pays yely 5s 4d [and] hold[es] in wyntt[er] 4 best[es] on horsse
8 harre townend hold[es] hawf a messe [and] hawf a noxgange
9 of land pays yerly 3s 10d [and] hold[es] 3 best[es] on horsse
10 thomas gantmyll hold[es] a messe a noxgange of land
11 pays 9s he hold[es] 6 best[es] 2 horsse
12 Robert Moxsson hold[es] a messe a noxgange of land
13 [and] 6 ac[res] of roddeland [and] pays 7s 6d

[1] *Half*
[2] *Land recently cleared and brought into cultivation*
[3] *8 beasts 2 horses*

g.
1   Ryght[1] worschypfull [and] to me Synguler good lady I r[e]com[m]ende me un to yow
2   Prayng yow <…> to sende me a Buck a wedynsday nexte com[m]yng Acordyng
3   to the p[ro]mysse that my Mast[er] [and] ye made at my laste beyng w[i]t[h] yow for a
4   specyall frende of myn schall be maryde on thursday nexte co[m]myng to
5   the wyche I have p[ro]mysyde a buck wherfor I pray yow that he be not
6   dispoyntyde and my s[er]vice schall be the mor redyer to yow at all tymys
7   w[i]t[h] the grace of god wyche have yow i[n] kepynge wryttyn i[n] haste the 18
8   Day of Jule

     By yowr s[er]vant Will[i]am Goldwyn

     Madam I pray yow to speck to my Mast[er] for the £16
     that ys dew un to me

[1] *Another yogh here, this time transcribed as 'g'*

h.
1   xviii die Julii a[nn]o sexto E[dwardi] sexti[1]
2   Art[i]clez of agrem[en]t betwe[e]n Martyn Hastingez esquier on theon[e] p[ar]te
     Geffrey
3   Mabbez on thether p[ar]te and R[i]chard Hoo on the thirde p[ar]te for [and] conc[er]
     ne[n]g
4   a certeyn mariage by the g[ra]ce of god to be had and solemn[i]zed between
5   Gilez Mabbez son to the said Geffrey and Elizabeth doughter to the said
6   R[i]chard in maner and forme followenge that is to say[2]

[1] *18 July 1552*
[2] *The agreement continues in the final chapter*

AND FINALLY …

Nuncupative will of Alexander Williams:
1   Memorandum that in the moneth of August in the yeare
2   of our Lord God 1628 and on or about the sixteenth
3   day of the same moneth as alsoe on or about the
4   <one an> twentieth day of the same moneth Alexander
5   williams of the parish of Saint Sepulchers w[it]hout
6   Newgate London Esquire being sicke and weake
7   in bodie but of perfect mynde [and] memory, and
8   having an intent to dispose of his temporall
9   estate did by word <…> of mouth utter and
10   declare his mynde [and] will in manner following
11   or used word[es] to the like effect vi[delice]t Speaking
12   unto and meaning his eldest sonne Anthonie
13   williams said All my estate whatsoever (my

14   debts paid) I doe give unto you my sonne
15   and doe make you my whole [and] onelie
16   executor w[hi]ch word[es] or the like in effect
17   were spoken [and] uttred by the said M[aste]r Alexander
18   williams hee being then of perfect mynde
19   [and] memory in the presence [and] hearing of
20   divers credible wittnesses vi[delicet]
Ben[jamin] Wallinger
Thomas Easton
signu[m] Andree Muncke

Letter to Richard Hoo:
1   After our co[m]mendac[i]ons wher as we have receyved the
2   Kinge [and] quenes ma[jes]ties co[m]myssyon dyrected unto us oute
3   of ther highnes Courte of the Chauncerie dated the
4   24ti of November last past aucthorysinge [and] appoyntinge
5   us Co[m]myssyon[er]s to exa[m]myne you and ev[er]ie of you
6   of or upon a certeyne bill and Interrogatories
7   annexed to the same, being exhybyted by thomas
8   Hoo as it shall more playnlie appeare unto you
9   These shalbe therfor to require you and nevertheles
10   by vertew of the said co[m]myssyon to co[m]maunde [and] charge
11   you and ev[er]ie of you to be and appeare before us
12   at Walsyngham upon Saterdaye beinge the 19th daye
13   of this Instaunte moneth of december next co[m]mynge
14   before 9th of the clocke in the Forenone of the same
15   daye to thentent that we may then and ther p[ro]sede
16   in the Kinge and quene ther ma[jes]ties said co[m]myssyon
17   accordinglie And that ye fayle not hereof as you [and]
18   ev[er]ie of you will awnswer to the contrarie at your
19   perill wrytten this 10th of december 1556

Letter, mid-fifteenth century:
1   Ryght worschypffull mayst[er] y reco[m]maunde me ev[er] mor[1] hartely unto your mayst[er]schyp
2   De[sir]yng you to und[e]rstande th[a]t y have done the message th[at] ye sent to me for
3   that ys to sey y have bowght for you 20ti hogges and the p[ri]s of 9 ys 16d
4   apease[2] and the p[ri]s 3 hogges 14d apease and the p[ri]s of 7 12d
5   apease and 1 Borpegge[3] p[ri]s 8d No more to you but Ihu[4] have you in
6   his kepynge and wretyn atte Wodefforde the Thorsdaye next aft[e]r Seynt Luke daye

[1] *It is not clear whether the mark at the end of this and other words, including 'your' in this line, signifies an abbreviation or not*

[2] *'and the price of nine is 16d apiece'*

[3] *Boar pig*

[4] *Another abbreviation for Jesus contracted from the Greek*

Copy of marriage certificate, September 1594:

   11° di[e] Septem[bris] a[nn]o 1594 Regn[i] Regine 36°[1]

1   On the day and yeare above wrytten were ioyned
2   together in ^holye^ matrimonie Francis Wollye and Marie Haw
3   trie according to the forme p[re]scribed in the booke of Co[m]men pray[e]r
4   by vertue of a License graunted by the L[ord] Archebysshopp
5   of Cant[erbury] dated 7° die mensis Septembris a[nn]o 1594 and ith
6   the p[re]sence of us whose names are undersubscribed and of
7   diverse other credible p[er]sons
     Wynifrede Pigott
     Jo[hn] Pigott
     George maynwaringe
     Rafe Latham

[1] *'On the 11th day of September in the 36th year of the reign of the queen 1594'*

Articles of agreement, 1552:
1   First that the seid mariage shalbe had [and] solemnised betwe[en] the seid
2   Gilez [and] Elizabeth before the feast of all saynctez next co[m]meng if the the[1]
3   p[ar]tiez will therunto assent [and] agree [and] the Lawez of the Chirche will it
     ordeigne[2]
4   It[e]m the seid Richard in considerac[i]on of the same mariage shall content [?]
5   [and] pay to the seid Gilez [and] Elizabeth foure score <...> and fyve markez
6   in forme foloweng that is to sey at the day of the mariage 20ti markes
7   and at Lammez which shalbe in the yere of oure Lord god a thousand
8   fyve hundred fiftie [and] thre other 20 markes and in the same feast then
9   next foloweng £15 and in the same feast then next foloweng
10   other £15 in full paym[en]t of the seid somme of fourescore [and] five markes

[1] *'the' written twice*
[2] *The 'n' is reduced to a line here and in several other words*

1   It[e]m the said Richard before seyd feast shall make unto the said
2   <Richard> Gilez [and] Elizabeth a goode [and] sure leez for terme of <...> 20ti yerez
3   from michal[mas] next co[m]meng Res[er]veng to the seid Richard [and] his heirez
4   sex poundez [and] fyveteen Shillingez. The rep[ar]ac[i]ons of the housez to be
5   susteyned [and] bore by the seid Gilez [and] Elizabeth in such wise as
6   his father Geffrey Mabbez hath hetherto borne [and] susteyned

1   it is agreed that the seid Richard w[i]t[h]in two yerez next aft[er]
2   the seid feast shall at his costez [and] charges <...> make or cause to be
3   made w[i]t[h] tymbre wurke an hous of thirtie foote in Length [and] in
4   breadeth 16 foote w[i]t[h]in the wallez ...

Appendix A: Glossary

A.1: Some General Terms

Abbreviations: Shortened forms of words and phrases used to save time, space and effort, and generally indicated by marks or symbols. By the eleventh century, the systematic abbreviation of Latin was fully developed, with four main classes of abbreviation:

Contraction: A form of abbreviation where marks indicate that one or more letters within a word have been omitted, so only the beginning and end of the word remain.

Suspension: A form of abbreviation where the beginning of the word is written and either a general or a specific mark indicates that the end is suppressed.

Special signs: Marks that either have an independent meaning, indicating that particular letters are missing, or have a relative meaning, depending on which letters they appear on or near.

Stacked or superscript letters: A form of contraction, where superior letters, as in M^r (Master), signify missing letters, of which the superscript letter is one.

Archives: Records selected for permanent preservation for their continuing value.

Book hands: Scripts used for library or liturgical manuscripts.

Caroline minuscule: The standard book script of Western Europe, developed at the end of the eighth century, and in use throughout the Holy Roman Empire until the beginning of the thirteenth century.

Copperplate: Writing made with a flexible, pointed metal pen using letter forms from copybooks printed from models engraved on copper.

Court hands: Scripts used for records, as opposed to the book hands used for manuscripts.

Cursive: Scripts written with either an edged or a flexible pointed pen, where most of the movements of the pen are recorded on the writing surface. Parts of individual letters are formed without lifting the pen, and the strokes are 'pulled', 'pushed' or 'sidled'. Letters may also be joined to the letters that follow.

Diplomatic: The study of the form, contents, production and authenticity of charters; now used for the study of manuscripts and records in general. Palaeography is a component of diplomatic.

Documentary hands: Cursive scripts used by clerks, scriveners and private correspondents for public and private records.

Documents: Materials bearing text providing information.

Formal: Scripts written with an edged pen, where individual letters are formed by pulled strokes with pen lifts. The scripts are therefore non-cursive, and mainly used in manuscripts rather than records.

Gothic: The system of scripts that developed from the Caroline minuscule between the twelfth and sixteenth centuries, and which were used through most of Western Europe. They were characterised by a hierarchy of book hands and documentary hands, and 'bastard' and 'hybrid' hands that combined features of both.

Hands: The scripts used by writers with their own distinguishing features and idiosyncrasies.

Humanistic: Scripts based on a 'rediscovered' Caroline minuscule that developed in Italy in the fifteenth century, where they replaced Gothic hands, and were adapted for use in written works from the Humanist movement (and therefore called 'humanistic scripts'); these scripts, rather than Gothic, became the basis of modern handwriting and modern book typefaces.

Manuscripts: Books or documents written by hand, usually on paper or parchment, rather than printed or typed.

Palaeography: The study of old handwriting, in order to read records and library manuscripts with accuracy, and to date, classify and localise handwriting.

Records: Information recorded in any form that provides evidence of business or personal activity.

Record type: A typeface used until the end of the nineteenth century, notably by the Record Commissioners, for the printing of the early nineteenth-century folio series such as the Statutes of the Realm, the Hundred Rolls, and in the publications of the Pipe Roll Society. Special marks were used in print to represent manuscript marks of abbreviation.

Scripts: Model systems of handwriting, each with distinctive style, forms and characteristics, governed by a set of rules, and belonging to a particular historical period or genre. In practice, 'script' and 'hand', which is the script as it is actually used by a writer, are often used interchangeably.

Scriveners: Professional writers belonging to a guild of men called '*scriptores littere curialis*', the 'writers of the court letter', who recorded business transactions from the mid-fourteenth century.

Transcriptions: Copies of texts.
   Diplomatic transcription: A reproduction of an original document as exactly as possible in text.
   Semi-diplomatic transcription: A reproduction of an original document in text that makes changes, following certain conventions, in the interests of clarity and readability.

A.2: English Documentary Hands

Anglicana: The name given by the palaeographer M.B. Parkes to the cursive book scripts that emerged in England in the mid-thirteenth century. There were several varieties of the script peculiar to English manuscripts and documents in the fourteenth and fifteenth centuries, but they share recognisable characteristics such as the two-compartment 'a' and 8-shaped 'g'. The documentary hands are often referred to as 'court' hands, and were current at the same time as secretary, which eventually predominated; however, anglicana letter forms may be found mixed with secretary letter forms well into the sixteenth century.

Bastard: Late medieval scripts that mix the forms and features of cursive scripts with book hands.

Chancery: The special style of handwriting used by Chancery clerks for the engrossing of letters patent and enrolments. Chancery emerged as a distinctive set hand towards the end of the fifteenth century and reached its high point towards the end of the sixteenth century. It was abolished by law in the eighteenth century, although it continued in use for the enrolment of Acts of Parliament into the nineteenth century.

Court: A term used for the hands adopted for the enrolments and registers of the central law courts at Westminster, but also used as a general term for the hands used for business records before the introduction of secretary, and for many legal documents until the early eighteenth century. The 'set' hands of the various courts and government departments became specialised during the course of the later fifteenth century and were abolished, along with the use of Latin, during the Commonwealth in 1651. Court hands returned with the restoration of the monarchy in 1660 but were abolished again with effect from 1733.

Engrossing: An upright and enlarged hand used for the final authoritative copy of legal documents onto parchment.

Exchequer: The special styles of handwriting used in the departments of the Exchequer. A distinctive style of writing developed in the twelfth century for the production of the Pipe Rolls and other enrolled accounts. Distinct scripts also developed in the fifteenth century for the Memoranda Rolls produced by the King's Remembrancer and by the Lord Treasurer's Remembrancer. The scripts were distinguished from Chancery hand by around 1530 and abolished by law in the eighteenth century.

Free: Name given by early twentieth-century palaeographers to medieval documentary hands, to distinguish the variety of hands written for everyday purposes from the hands used in the courts and government departments.

Glossing: A script, usually italic, used for commentary or headings within a document.

Hybrid: Late medieval scripts where the forms and features of book hands were fused with cursive elements.

Italic: A general heading for the humanistic varieties of script that developed in Italy in the fifteenth century following a major reform of handwriting as a return to 'Roman simplicity'. Italic made its way to England, where it was associated with the royal court and became the preferred educated hand from the mid-sixteenth century. It was used in England for documents written in Latin, and as a glossing hand for documents written in English, for quoted matter, and for headings and marginalia from the early to mid-sixteenth century. It was used as an alternative to secretary from the early seventeenth century and soon displaced it completely. Few abbreviations were used, apart from superscript letters.

Legal: The special court hand used for the Plea Rolls, and writs in the central law courts and the courts of Common Pleas and King's Bench. The term is also used for the hands used by lawyers and clerks outside of the central courts for a variety of personal and business documents such as private letters, deeds and court rolls.

Mixed: Until the end of the sixteenth century, scripts were generally distinct, with secretary used for the body of text and writings in English in general, and italic for quotations and headings and writings in Latin; thereafter, scripts were mixed, either with a mix of italic letter forms in mainly secretary hands, or a mix of secretary letter forms persisting in mainly italic hands. By the mid-seventeenth century, mixed hands had mainly died out, with only secretary 'e', 'h' and 'r' forms remaining. Mixed hands are very common and long-lived in legal series such as Chancery proceedings, which did not use the special legal hands.

Round: By the early eighteenth century, italic and secretary had fused into the English national round hand, characterised by a slope to the right and linking loops. It was the dominant documentary hand from around 1725. From the early eighteenth century, a clear distinction was made for the first time between the letters 'i' and 'j', and 'u' and 'v'. From the end of the eighteenth century, a system of ties and links joined all letters in words for the first time, and handwriting had taken on much of the appearance of modern handwriting.

Secretary: A cursive script used for general business purposes when writing in English. It was a development of an Italian notarial script probably imported from France and was extensively used in ecclesiastical registers and Chancery warrants from the 1370s. It developed alongside anglicana, was widespread from the mid-fifteenth century, and was the principal script of England by the sixteenth century. Many Tudor secretary letter forms are unlike their anglicana counterparts and are also unlike the letter forms that are used today, making it harder to read than both earlier and later hands. Secretary was perfected by English writing masters in the later sixteenth century, and rapidly disappeared after the second quarter of the seventeenth century, although some of the characteristic letter forms persisted into the eighteenth century.

Set: The individual writing styles adopted by the various courts and departments of central government for important business such as enrolments. Over the course of the fifteenth century the hands written in different departments developed characteristics that marked them off from one another, and all new entrants to Chancery, the central law courts and the departments of the Exchequer were instructed in its set hand. This led to a uniformity in the writing of the records of that department and differentiated it from other departments. Set hands were distinctive rather than legible, particularly at later dates; legal hands were almost illegible to anyone outside their departments by the end of the seventeenth century. Set hands ceased to be written in 1733. 'Set' may also refer to an ideal script, written as a writing master taught it.

For a description of the different hands in use in England from 1066 to the present, see especially L.C. Hector, *The Handwriting of English Documents*. The evolution of scripts from ancient times to the early modern period is traced in M.P. Brown, *A Guide to Western Historical Scripts from Antiquity to 1600*, and N. Denholm-Young, *Handwriting in England and Wales*, and in both books the major phases in the development of scripts are illustrated with full-page plates with commentaries and transcriptions. M.B. Parkes, who coined the term 'anglicana', traces its evolution and varieties in the fourteenth and fifteenth centuries, in *English Cursive Book Hands, 1250–1500*.

A.3: Terms Used to Describe Handwriting

The simplest way to introduce some commonly used handwriting terminology is by reference to a diagram:

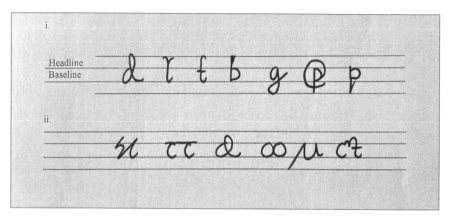

Figure A.1: Elements of script.

Ascender: The part of the letter that extends beyond the headline. Ascenders may be looped, as in the letter 'd' in Figure A.1i above, split or forked, as in the letter 'l', hooked, as in the letter 't', or clubbed, as in the letter 'b'.

Aspect: The general appearance of handwriting and its main characteristics.

Bowl: The closed, curved stroke appended to the stem of letters such as 'd' and 'p'; also known as the lobe.

Brevigraph: An abbreviation in which two or more letters are represented by a single symbol. For example, the 'p' in Figure A.1i with a curl cutting through the descender, which represents 'pro'.

Broken stroke: A writing movement in which the direction of the pen is changed suddenly without being lifted from the page. This is common in secretary letters, such as the small 'a', the first letter in Figure A.1ii above, where the usual bowl is replaced by a broken stroke.

Conjoined letters: A type of ligature where two adjoining letters contain between them one stroke that belongs to both. In Figure A.1ii above, one crossbar is used for both letters 'cc'. In 'ae' and 'oo' the usual tie is omitted, and the letters are 'twinned'; these are also known as digraphs. It is common to see 'pp' with one head for both letters; with the secretary long 'ss', the final descender is often omitted.

Descender: The part of the letter that extends below the baseline. Descenders may be looped, as in the letter 'g' in Figure A.1i above.

Double-length letter: A letter, such as 'f', with the stroke extending both above the headline and below the baseline.

Duct: The distinctive way in which letters are written in a particular hand, affected among other things by the size and cut of the nib, the angle at which the pen is held, the degree of pressure applied, the direction in which the pen is moved and the sequence of strokes creating the letters.

Graph: A letter made by one or more strokes.

Infralineal approach stroke: An approach stroke to a letter that begins below the baseline, as in the 'u' in Figure A.1ii above.

Infralinear letter: A letter, such as 'p', with a descender.

Ligature: Two letters joined in a special way that involves the modification of one or both letters. There are two types of ligature: conjoined letters and two letters joined by an added stroke that is not a continuation of part of the first letter. The added stroke is typically a curve or a loop from the top of the first letter to the top of the second letter, as in the 'ct' in Figure A.1ii.

Limb: The open, curved stroke appended to the stem of letters such as 'h' and 'n'.

Linear letter: A letter, such as 'a', that fits between the baseline and the headline.

Link: A stroke that is the continuation of some part of one letter and joins it to the following letter.

Loop: Curved shape in which the line returns to its point of departure (as in the 'd' in Figure A.1i) or near to its point of departure (as in the 'g' in Figure A.1i).

Majuscule: Early book hand scripts, in which all letters are of equal height and written between two imaginary lines. The word also refers to capital as opposed to small letters, which in print are called upper case letters.

Minim: The short vertical strokes of letters such as 'i', 'm' and 'n'; the simplest letter, the 'i', consists of one minim.

Minuscule: A script in which some parts of some letters are taller or longer than others, but all fall between four imaginary lines, as in Figure A.1. All documentary scripts are minuscule. The word also refers to small as opposed to capital letters, which in print are called lower-case letters.

Otiose stroke: A decorative flourish, which does not form part of the letter or indicate an abbreviation.

Serif: A short decorative stroke projecting from the head or foot of a letter, which begins or ends the pen stroke, as in the 'p' in Figure A.1i.

Shading: The different thicknesses of stroke, depending largely on the position in which the pen is held.

Shaft: The single vertical stroke of letters such as 'k' and 't', forming the stem of the letter.

Slant: The degree of variation from the vertical of the minims.

Stem: The main vertical stroke of letters from which the whole letter is formed. Depending on the letter, the stem may be a minim stroke, or a shaft.

Stroke: A single trace of the pen on the page made without change of direction. Straight horizontal lines are known as head-strokes (the horizontal stroke at the top of a letter such as a capital 'T'), cross-strokes (such as the stroke that cuts through a small 't'), or base-strokes (such as the horizontal stroke at the bottom of capital 'L').

Supralinear letter: A letter, such as 'd' and 't', with an ascender.

Tie: A stroke connecting one part of a letter with another.

A.4: Descriptions of Different Letter Forms

Many letters had distinct forms, which have been given descriptive names that are used in manuscript studies in discussions about script:

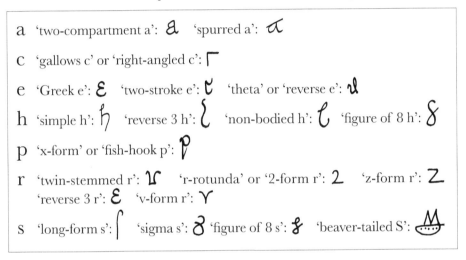

Figure A.2: Descriptive names for different letter forms.

For further terms describing features of writing and letter forms, see Cambridge University, Faculty of English, *English Handwriting Online*.

Appendix B:
Transcription Conventions

There are no hard and fast rules of transcription, even for the purpose of record publication. However, even when transcribing for the simple purpose of accessing content, it is good practice to follow certain conventions of presentation.

For transcriptions in English:

- Number the lines in the transcription, and retain the lineation, punctuation, capitalisations and spellings of the original.
- Do not expand the common abbreviations for pounds, shillings, pence; transcribe as £, s, d.
- Replace Roman numerals with Arabic numerals.
- Lower superscript letters.
- Expand abbreviations, extending marks and symbols as shown in Appendix D, encasing the expansions in square brackets.
- Silently replace the runic thorn Þ with 'th', the middle-English yogh 3 with 'g' or 'y' as appropriate.
- Enclose text that has been deleted within angle brackets <...>.
- Enclose text that has been interlined within carat marks ^...^.
- Where text is illegible, missing or blank, show as {...}.
- Place contextual notes, modern spelling or interpretative text that has been added by the transcriber in notes numbered within square brackets.

For transcriptions in Latin, it may be useful to make a full diplomatic transcription first, numbering the lines in the transcription and copying all abbreviation marks and special symbols. When satisfied with this, make a semi-diplomatic copy, following the above conventions, but:

- Retain Roman numerals.
- Use an apostrophe to indicate unknown or uncertain endings, for example where a place name has variant forms (for example, Oxonia/Oxonium/Oxefordia/Oxenforda for Oxford), or where a mark of abbreviation is otiose.

For translations from Latin into English:

- Modernise place names if it is clear what place is intended; otherwise, leave the name as spelt in the document.
- Anglicise Latin forenames.
- With surnames, retain the spelling and keep 'le' and 'de' as part of the name, unless it is clear that the name is a Latin translation of an English name (see the list of Latin forms of English surnames in *The Record Interpreter*).
- With place names or words written in English in a Latin document, replace 'le' with 'the'.
- Replace Roman numerals with Arabic numerals.

These conventions are guidelines only (and different scholars follow different conventions). The usual practice for typescript transcriptions is to extend abbreviations in italics, rather than enclose in square brackets. When transcribing documents for publication, refer to P.D.A. Harvey, *Editing Historical Records*. For conventions used in full diplomatic transcriptions, see M.P. Brown, *A Guide to Western Historical Scripts from Antiquity to 1600*.

Appendix C: Typical Letter Forms

Two alphabets have been constructed from an examination of the handwriting in hundreds of documents to illustrate the characteristic letter forms used over time in English records.

The first alphabet, shown in C.1, covers the letter forms of the secretary hand, one of the main classes of script in general use in England from the fifteenth century. The letters are in rough chronological order, starting with the letter forms that predominated during the fifteenth and early sixteenth centuries. These are followed by Elizabethan secretary and less common later letter forms, where they differ from the earlier forms.

Elizabethan secretary was characterised by a wide range of forms – in particular, several different types of 'e', 'h', 'r' and 's', often within a single document. Most of the letter forms of the second main class of script, italic, are not included because they are generally instantly recognisable from modern letter forms. The large majority of documents of interest to family historians will be written in secretary or italic scripts, or a mixture of the two.

The second alphabet, shown in C.2, covers the letter forms of the third class of script, the court hands, which were in use in England from the mid-thirteenth century to the end of the fifteenth century, and also in the central courts and as general law hands until the early eighteenth century. Typical 'anglicana' letter forms, again in a rough chronological order, are followed by the letter forms of the legal hands used in the Courts of Common Pleas and King's Bench, then Chancery letter forms. Exchequer letter forms are not set out separately. King's Remembrancer's hand was similar in style to Chancery, and Lord Treasurer's Remembrancer's hand was similar in style to the legal hand.

No attempt has been made to reflect the distinctive way in which letters were written with a reed or quill pen on parchment or vellum, which varied considerably over time and between individuals. Furthermore, there was always a considerable amount of individual variation and deviation from normal letter patterns. The aim here is to provide tables of the different basic letter forms; every letter in any document found in English archives from the mid-thirteenth century to the end of the nineteenth century should be recognisable either as one of these variant forms, or as a variant of a modern letter form.

Capital letters reflected individual idiosyncrasies to a greater extent than small letters, and forms varied a great deal. They were often decorated with ornamental vertical or oblique strokes through the middle, and with dots in the loops of letters. The alphabets in C.1 and C.2 show the commoner forms of capital letters. Some capital letters – particularly 'E', 'G', 'I', 'S' and 'W' – have so many unusual varieties that they can only really be identified by context.

Anglicana capitals persisted into the later sixteenth century and beyond, and many forms are very unlike letters that we are now familiar with. Check both C.1 and C.2 for unrecognisable capital letters.

Further Resources

For a discussion of the characteristics of documentary hands, with exemplary plates and transcripts, see L.C. Hector, *The Handwriting of English Documents*, Chapter V. There are several plates with useful commentaries on the characteristics of handwriting, punctuation and abbreviation in literary texts in A.G. Petti, *English Literary Hands from Chaucer to Dryden*, along with a useful guide to terminology.

C.1: Secretary Hand Letter Forms

	Fifteenth century to early sixteenth century	Elizabethan Tudor and later
a		
b		
c		
d		
e		
f		
g		
h		
ij		
k		
l		
m		
n		
o		
p		
q		
r		
s		
t		
uv		
w		
x		
y		
z		

| A |
| B |
| C |
| D |
| E |
| F |
| G |
| H |
| IJ |
| K |
| L |
| M |
| N |
| O |
| P |
| Q |
| R |
| S |
| T |
| UV |
| W |
| X |
| Y |
| Z |

C.2: Court Hand Letter Forms

	Anglicana				Legal			Chancery		
a										
b										
c										
d										
e										
f										
g										
h										
i j										
k										
l										
m										
n										
o										
p										
q										
r										
s										
t										
u v										
w										
x										
y										
z										

	Anglicana				Legal			Chancery		
A										
B										
C										
D										
E										
F										
G										
H										
IJ										
K										
L										
M										
N										
O										
P										
Q										
R										
S										
T										
UV										
W										
X										
Y										
Z										

Appendix D:
Marks of Abbreviation, Punctuation and Correction

D.1: Marks of Abbreviation: English

In writing in English, abbreviation was managed in two ways: by the use of a few general and special marks carried over from the writing of medieval Latin, and used in the same way or extended, and by the use of superior, usually terminal, letters.

GENERAL MARKS OF ABBREVIATION
These were indicated by:
A point or colon used at the end of a word, for example:

Tho: Tho[mas]   L. L[ordship]

A straight, curved or wavy horizontal stroke above letters or through ascenders, an apostrophe, or an upward backward curve, or downward curve, from the final letter, to avoid taking up the pen, for example:

ī i[n]   Ric? Ric[hard]   Wm̃ or Witt W[illia]m or Will[iam]

These general marks, particularly a horizontal stroke through every final double 'l', and the extension of the last strokes of final letters, were often otiose.

SPECIAL MARKS OF ABBREVIATION
A few special marks, or brevigraphs, were used that had a particular meaning:

ʄ ℓ 'es', 'is', 's'   ʒ 'et'; or 'ue' after the letter 'q'
ʔ 'ior', 'er', 'ir' 'or', 'ur'   ₰ ƒ 'sir' or 'sar'   ᕯ -'con'
ℰ ℓ & ƭ ℓ ὲ ɣ ℓ ƻ ℬ some of the many abbreviations for 'and'
ℓͭ &c 'et cetera'

ABBREVIATION INDICATED BY SUPERIOR LETTERS

Final raised superior letters were used to indicate an omission of which the letters were part, for example:

wth w[i]th M^r M[aste]r K^t K[nigh]t

Note also:

Some common Latin words were abbreviated and used in documents written in English:

$A^o D^{ni}$ A[nn]o D[omi]ni ('in the year of the lord')

$q3$ q[ue] (usually in 'annoque', ie: 'and in the year')

Figure 2.Cb Court hand capital letters.

$vi3$ vi[delicet] ('namely')

li s d abbreviations of the Latin words for pounds, shillings and pence (librae, solidi, denarii), generally written as superior letters

The following letter modifications were used in words starting with 'p':

ꝑ ꝓ words beginning with 'per' or 'par'

ꝑ p³ pᵉ words beginning with 'pre'

ꝑ ꝓ words beginning with 'pro'

Two special letters were used in English: the Anglo-Saxon letter thorn þ used to represent the letters 'th', which was gradually assimilated to y, as in yᵉ (the) and yᵗ (that); and the middle-English character yogh 3 used for 'g', 'gh', 'y', or 'w', as in, for example, 3ate (gate) or 3early (yearly); by the fifteenth century it was indistinguishable from the cursive letter 'z'.

The first letters of the word 'Christ' in Greek, the 'chi rho' (xp), were often used to begin words such as Christian, Christ, and Christopher.

D.2: Marks of Abbreviation: Latin

There were a handful of general marks of suspension and contraction, which probably cover around half of the abbreviations that are likely to be encountered, and some special marks and symbols and special abbreviations of common words.

ABBREVIATION WITH NO MARK

This might be a single letter, or a whole phrase. Where one letter stands for the whole word, this was usually the name of a monarch or important individual, or a word very commonly used, such as 'e' for 'est' or 'T' for 'testibus'. The single letters signifying common words might also be marked off by points, such as '.i.' for 'id est' or '.n.' for 'enim'. In addition, many common words and phrases were abbreviated with no mark, for example, 'het' for 'habet', 'huit' for 'habuit', 'it' for 'item', and 'io in mia' for 'ideo in misericordia'.

GENERAL MARKS OF ABBREVIATION

General marks of suspension, indicating the omission of a final letter or letters, were common at all periods, taking the form of:

1. A straight, curved, wavy, looped or ornamented bar above letters such as ⎯∼∪∧∩∝ as for example in: c̄ū cu[m] c̃õm̃ com[itatus]

2. An extension upward and backward, or downward, of the terminal letter, an apostrophe, or a line through a terminal ascender or ascenders, for example *man* man[erium] or *hab ent* or *hab endy* habend[um] *exis ƚ* exist[it]

3. A very small curl on the final letter, for example *capi ƚ* capit[e]

4. Sometimes special abbreviation marks (see below) were also used as general suspension marks:
   e & ꝛ ꝩ ꝫ ƺ

There were also general marks of contraction, indicating the omission of letters in the middle of a word, taking the form of:

1. A straight, curved, wavy, looped or ornamented bar above a letter, which may pass through an ascender, for example:
   o̅m̅s om[ne]s *e̅c̅* e[ss]e *d̄na* d[omi]na *batt io* balli[v]o
   Joh es Joh[ann]es

2. A vertical wavy line like a narrow 's', or a backward curve, at the end of a word or in the middle of a word, to indicate an earlier omission, for example:
   arm igi' armig[er]i *ml�futb̄o* m[u]lto

SPECIAL MARKS OF ABBREVIATION

There were also several special marks of suspension and contraction, each with a particular meaning of its own:

1. A straight line or wavy line over a vowel indicates the omission of 'm' or 'n' following the vowel, for example:

   ī i[n]   ūde u[n]de

2. A vertical wavy line above a word like a narrow 's', a backward curve, or a shape looking like a number 7 { S ʔ ʅ ♪ ⁊ indicates the omission of 'er' or 're', for example:

   ♡ versus   pon·er⁷ ponere   tˢra tʳra tˢra tˀra t[er]ra

3. The sign ↑ ℰ at the end of a word represents 'is', 'es'; it may also be used as a general mark of suspension as in ℞ R[ex] or R[ecipe].

4. The sign ꝫ Ʒ at the end of a word, on the line of writing indicates 'us' following the letter 'b', or 'ue' following the letter 'q'; it is also a general mark of suspension in common words such as libet, licet, sed, debet and, very commonly, videlicet viƷ.

5. The '2-shaped r', which may be very squashed and look like a cursive 'a':

   ꝛ above the line of writing indicates 'ur', or any third-person singular passive verb ending ('tur', 'atur' 'itur' etc.).

   ꝛ̵ at the end of a word on the line of writing, and cut with a general abbreviation mark, indicates the genitive plural 'rum', or 'run', 'ran', 'ras', 'res', 'ris'; or acts as a general suspension mark.

6. The following signs ꝯ ꝰ Ʒ ꝗ ꝝ:

   placed at the beginning of middle of a word, on the line of writing, indicate 'cum', 'cog', 'con', 'com', 'cun'

   placed at the end or middle of a word, above the line of writing, indicate 'us', 'ius', 'os', 'ost'.

'P' MODIFICATIONS

A line through the descender, or a loop starting from the bottom of the descender indicates 'per', 'par', 'por':

A variety of backward curves or lines following or above the letter indicate 'pre':

A loop cutting through the descender indicates 'pro':

A flourish above the line after a letter indicates 'post':

'Q' MODIFICATIONS:

All of the common words beginning with the letter 'q' will be found in abbreviated form, for example:

que   qui

quia   quando

quam   quorum

quod   quoque   quoniam

ABBREVIATION BY SUPERIOR LETTER

This may have a particular meaning, as below, or be used to save space with no abbreviation purpose.

A superior letter indicates an omission, frequently of the letter 'r', of which the superior letter forms a part, such as:

ci[r]cum   pa[r]te   cont[r]a

In some common words, the superior letter may be directly above the first letter, for example:

nec   vero   mihi   sibi   nihil   erga   ubi   igitur

OTHER COMMON ABBREVIATIONS

⊘ ℯ ℯ 2 7 ᴧ ℤ ℩ ℈ ℳ some of the many abbreviations of 'et'; and as an abbreviation for 'etiam' when surmounted by a straight, curved or wavy horizontal line, for example $\widehat{7}$:

e^+ e^r ℩ ℞ $c^ε$ e^t ℰ some of the many abbreviations of 'et cetera'

ϐ ♌ ℔ ♉ ϐ ℥ ser

ϸ sis, sus

ex^e ex parte

Ȝ ÷ ÷ (rarely seen after the end of the twelfth century)

Words containing 'Christ' were often abbreviated using the initial Greek letters of the words Jesus or Christ, for example:

$\overline{Jhc}$ $\overline{xpc}$ $\overline{Jhs}$ $\overline{ihs}$ $\overline{xps}$

An abbreviation for 'Christi' is ẋ

D.3: Punctuation and Correction Marks

In formal medieval documents, only two forms of punctuation were used: the point (full stop), and the medieval comma, which looks like an inverted semi-colon:

ᴗ ✓

Punctuation was almost completely absent from English legal documents by the early fifteenth century, and minimal thereafter, but for other purposes several signs of punctuation emerged over the centuries, and by the mid-sixteenth century, all the main modern marks used in documents (point, comma, colon, semi-colon, question mark, parentheses, horizontal dash, quotation marks, apostrophe) were known. The virgule, a short oblique line, was also used, often taking the place of other punctuation marks. However, the use of capital letters and punctuation marks was unsystematic, with documents often exhibiting extremes of punctuation, from a complete absence to an indiscriminate use of marks throughout.

The point, often placed above the line of writing, usually marked the end of a sentence, but was often also used for other purposes, for example, to separate numerals and single-letter abbreviations of words and names from other words in a sentence; to act as a mark of abbreviation; to dot the 'y' to distinguish it from the thorn; and to dot the 'i' to distinguish it from other minims.

Until the end of the sixteenth century, but not much after, the comma often took the form of the virgule, sometimes with points either side of it: ⫶

This often took the place of other punctuation marks and was the most common indication of a break until the mid-sixteenth century when the comma came into general use.

Colons were used more commonly than today and were also used as a mark of abbreviation.

The semi-colon, which appeared in the second half of the sixteenth century, marked a pause longer than a comma, and along with the earlier reversed semi-colon also took the place of other punctuation marks.

The question mark was often obliquely angled to the line of writing, looking like an inverted semi-colon: ⟋ ⟍

Brackets were used from the sixteenth century to enclose parenthetical material, or to take the function now given to inverted commas.

The main function of the hyphen was to indicate where a word was broken at the end of a line, although often words continued on to the next line with no mark at all; a double hyphen became common in the sixteenth and seventeenth centuries.

The apostrophe, which was a simplified version of the 'er' brevigraph ⟋, was used in the modern sense as an indication of the possessive from the seventeenth century; until then, the 'es' brevigraph ℯ was commonly used.

By the eighteenth century, punctuation had assumed the grammatical function that it has today, and capitalisation and spelling were largely normalised.

It is important to distinguish between marks that were intended as punctuation, and marks that serve other purposes such as line-fillers (strokes to fill space at end of line of writing), paraphs (decorative flourishes associated with personal signatures), flourishes to fill space, and paragraph or marks for subdivisions of lines such as the following, as these marks do not form part of the semi-diplomatic transcription:

⟨ cc ʃʃ ʃ ⟩

Where a mistake had been made, the writer might:

- erase the error (scrape the surface and write over it)
- cancel the error (cross out words, or draw criss-cross lines across a passage, and write in the alterations in the margin)

- expunge or underscore the error (place dots or a line under the unwanted letters or words to be altered)
- obliterate the error (ink out or otherwise obscure the whole error).

Letters could also be altered by superimposing or superscribing correct letters over the deleted ones. The method of correction is noted in diplomatic transcriptions, but in a semi-diplomatic transcription, it is only necessary to note that a correction had been made (see Appendix B, Transcription Conventions).

Where an omission had been made, this was usually indicated by a mark such as a caret (^) or virgule (although the mark was often forgotten), with the omitted matter inserted between lines, or by a mark that was then duplicated in the margin where the omitted matter was inserted.

For a detailed treatment of marks of punctuation and manuscript corrections, see A.G. Petti's *English Literary Hands from Chaucer to Dryden*, and Chapter 6 of Raymond Clemens and Timothy Graham's *Introduction to Manuscript Studies*. *The Handwriting of English Documents* by L.C. Hector is an invaluable reference book on abbreviation, punctuation and correction.

Appendix E:
Numbers: Numerals,
Money and Dates

Numerals

The Roman numerals i (1), v (5), x (10), L (50), C (100), D (500) and M (1000) were commonly used in documents until the sixteenth century in much the same way that they are still occasionally used today. The last 'i' in a sequence took the 'i-longa' form (transcribed as 'j'), and iiij was used instead of iv for the number 4. One half was represented by the letters 'di' ('dimidia', half in Latin).

As counting was done in scores, it is common to find large numbers expressed as multiples of twenty, for example, ij threescore, or sixty. By the same method, V^c may be used instead of D for five hundred, and V^m for five thousand, and so on. A horizontal stroke over a Roman numeral was also used for 'mille', so $\overline{iij}$ indicates the number three thousand.

Arabic numerals were used as alternatives to Roman numerals from the end of the thirteenth century, and were widely used from the sixteenth century, but are not always instantly recognisable:

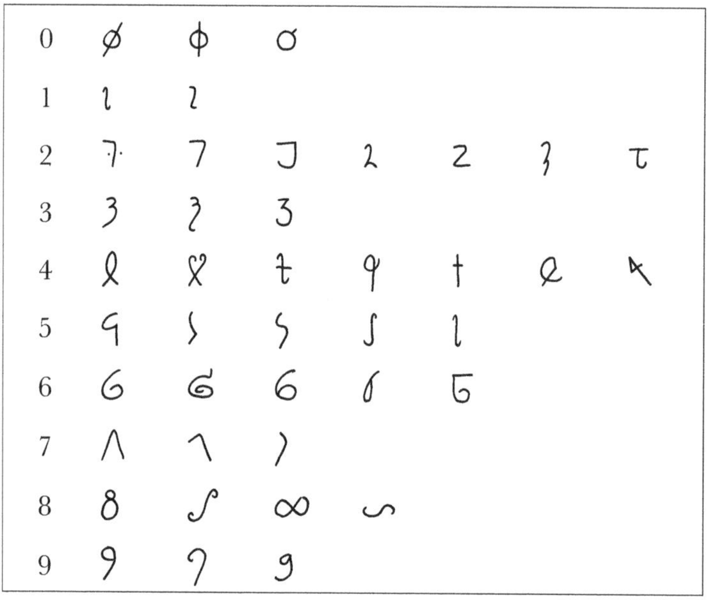

Figure E.1: Arabic numerals.

For medieval arithmetic and Arabic numerals in the medieval period, see L.C. Hector, *The Handwriting of English Documents*, Chapter IV.

Money

Before decimalisation, the currency denominations were pence, shillings and pounds. These were indicated by the superscript letters 'd' (denarius), 's' (solidus), which was worth 12 pennies, and 'l' or 'li' (libra), which was worth 20 shillings or 240 pennies. In addition, the superscript letters 'qu' (quadrans or quarta) for a farthing, worth a quarter of a penny, and 'ob' (obolus) for a halfpenny will be found. It is also common to find references to the groat (worth 4 pennies), the florin (worth 2 shillings), the crown (worth 5 shillings), the guinea (worth 21 shillings), and the sovereign (worth £1, or 20 shillings). The mark, which was often used in valuations, was not a coin, but was worth 13s 4d, or 160 pennies.

By the nineteenth century, the superscript 's' for 'solidus' that was used for shillings had evolved into an oblique vertical line; for example, we find 2/6 instead of 2^{s}6^d.

Dates

Dates may be given in three ways: using the day, month and calendar year in the modern form in words or numerals; by using the day and month and the year of the monarch's reign (regnal year) rather than the calendar year; and by a day in the church year rather than the calendar day and month.

CALENDAR YEAR

A papal bull decreed that the 'new style' Gregorian calendar should replace the 'old-style' Julian calendar in 1582, with ten days dropped to allow the calendar year to catch up with the solar year. This took place in much of Catholic Europe in 1582 and 1583, but in Orthodox and Protestant areas the calendar was replaced at different dates into the twentieth century.

England, Ireland and Scotland adopted the Gregorian calendar in 1752, with Wednesday, 2 September being followed by Thursday, 14 September. In England, the start of the legal year was also moved to 1 January in the same year. In Scotland, it had already taken place in 1600, though the Julian calendar was used until 1752.

Before 1752 in England, the calendar year began on Lady Day, 25 March. When reporting historical events that took place before 1752, it is usual practice to use the date recorded at the time of the event, adjusting the year to start on 1 January. Dates were often given a double indication in records, for example '5 March 1710/11'. If the double indication had not been given, and the date read 5 March 1710, the date would need to be modernised to 1711 in the transcription. Diplomatic letters between the Continent and England often employed dates in both the Julian and Gregorian calendars.

Note that, because March was historically the first month of the year, September was literally the seventh month of the year, October the eighth, and so on. As these months retained their names after the calendar year was changed (and September became the ninth month and so on) the following abbreviations will still be found after 1752:

7ber (September), 8ber (October), 9ber (November),
10ber or xber (December).

REGNAL YEAR

Dating by regnal year was often used instead of, or as well as, dating by calendar year. The regnal year of each monarch began on the day that the previous monarch died. Thus, Victoria's reign began on 20 June 1837, the day that William IV died, giving her a regnal year of 20 June–19 June, and ended with her death on 22 January 1901, when Edward VII's reign began.

To convert a regnal year to a calendar year, use Table 2/II, 'Regnal Years of Rulers from AD 1154', in Cheney's *A Handbook of Dates for Students of British History*. For example, for 1 March 17 James I, referring to the table, the seventeenth year of James I's reign runs from 24 March 1619 to 23 March 1620, so the date is 1 March 1620. Dates in the handbook are 'new style', so do not have to be further adjusted as above.

CHURCH YEAR

Before the sixteenth century, dates of the religious year were often used in place of the day and month. Where a saint's day is used, it is a simple matter to convert the date to modern form. To find the date, for example of St Catherine's Day 14 Edward II, use Table 4/1 in Cheney's *A Handbook of Dates for Students of British History* to find St Catherine's Day (25 November), then Table 2/II to find 14 Edward II (8 July 1320–7 July 1321). The date is therefore 25 November 1320. If the day was a moveable feast, however, it is necessary to also find the date of Easter to convert the date to modern form. So, for example, to find the date of Passion Sunday in the regnal year 14 Edward II, the entry in Table 2/II in Cheney's *A Handbook of Dates for Students of British History* refers the reader to Table 8/29, which gives the calendar for years (such as 1321) with an Easter Day of 19 April; Passion Sunday, 14 Edward II is shown to be 5 April 1321.

Measures

The booklet *How Heavy, How Much and How Long?* by Colin R. Chapman is indispensable both for recognising the names used to describe quantities of different materials or different measurements, and for the tables converting them into standardised measures. It covers general numeration, including the compound symbols used with Roman numerals; linear measurements, such as rod, furlong, nail, ell and bundle; square measurements, such as hide, oxgang and acre; cubic measurements, such as board, cast, peck, sack and firkin; weights, such as ounce, fotmal, bushel, load, last and pack; and money, covering coinages from the ninth century to decimalisation.

Sources

Bailey, Mark, *The English Manor* c.*1200–*c.*1500* (2002).

Bannerman, W. Bruce (ed.), *The Registers of St Martin Outwich London 1670–1873*, Harleian Society, Volume 32 (1905).

Beal, Peter, *A Dictionary of English Manuscript Terminology 1450–2000* (2008).

Bristow, Joy, *The Local Historian's Glossary of Words and Terms*, 3rd edition (2001).

Brown, Michelle P., *A Guide to Western Historical Scripts from Antiquity to 1600* (1990).

Chaplais, Pierre, *English Medieval Diplomatic Practice*, two volumes (1982).

Chapman, Colin R., *How Heavy, How Much and How Long? Weights, Money and Other Measures Used by our Ancestors* (1995).

Cheney, C.R., revised Jones, M., *A Handbook of Dates for Students of British History*, revised edition (2000).

Dawson, Giles E. and Kennedy-Skipton, Laetitia, *Elizabethan Handwriting 1500–1650*, 2nd edition (1981).

Denholm-Young, N., *Handwriting in England and Wales* (1954).

Emmison, F.G., *How to Read Local Archives 1550–1700* (1973).

Emmison, F.G., *Elizabethan Life: Home, Work and Land* (1976).

Forrest, Mark, *Reading Early Handwriting 1500–1700* (2019).

Gooder, Eileen A., *Latin for Local History*, 2nd edition (1978).

Grieve, Hilda E.P., *Examples of English Handwriting 1150–1750* (1954).

Hall, Hubert, *A Formula Book of English Official Historical Documents* (1908, reprinted 2006).

Halliwell, J.O., *A Handbook of Archaic and Provincial Words*, 7th edition (1872).

Harvey, P.D.A. (ed.), *Manorial Records of Cuxham, Oxfordshire circa 1200–1359* (1976).

Haydon, Edwin and Harrop, John (eds.), *Widworthy Manorial Court Rolls 1453–1617* (1997).

Hector, L.C., *The Handwriting of English Documents* (1958).

Hoskin, P.M., Slinn, S.L. and C.C. Webb, *Reading the Past: Sixteenth and Seventeenth-Century English Handwriting* (2001).

Jenkinson, H., *The Later Court Hands in England, from the Fifteenth Century to the Seventeenth Century*, two volumes (1927).

Johnson, C. and H. Jenkinson, *English Court Hand AD 1066 to 1500*, two volumes (1915).

Latham, R.E., *Revised Medieval Latin Word-List from British and Irish Sources* (1965).

Little, W., Fowler, H.W. and J. Coulson, *The Shorter Oxford English Dictionary*, two volumes (1933).

London Borough of Sutton Libraries and Arts Services, *Courts of the Manors of Beddington and Bandon 1498–1552*, transcribed and translated by Hedley Marne Gowans, edited by Michael Wilks and Jennifer Bray (1982).

London County Council, *Court Rolls of Tooting Beck Manor*, Volume I (1909).

Marshall, Hilary, *Palaeography for Family and Local Historians* (2004).

Martin, Charles Trice, *The Record Interpreter*, facsimile of 2nd edition (1982).

Milward, Rosemary, *A Glossary of Household, Farming and Trade Terms from Probate Inventories*, 2nd edition (1982).

Munby, Lionel, *Reading Tudor and Stuart Handwriting* (1988).

Newton, K.C., *Medieval Local Records. A Reading Aid* (1971).

Parkes, M.B., *English Cursive Book Hands 1250–1500* (1979).

Petti, Anthony G., *English Literary Hands from Chaucer to Dryden* (1977).

Poos, L.P. and Lloyd Bonfield (eds), *Select Cases in Manorial Courts 1250–1550* (Selden Society, 1998).

Raymond, Stuart A., *Words from Wills and Other Probate Records 1500–1800* (2004).

Steer, Francis W., *Farm and Cottage Inventories of Mid-Essex 1635–1749*, 2nd edition (1969).

Stuart, Denis, *Manorial Records* (1992).

Surrey Record Society, *Surrey Probate Inventories, 1558–1603*, Volume xxxix (2005).

Wimbledon Common Committee, *Extracts from the Court Rolls of the Manor of Wimbledon, Extending from 1 Edward IV to AD 1864* (1866).

Wright, J., *The English Dialect Dictionary* (1898–1905), six volumes.

Online Resources

British Academy, *Dictionary of Medieval Latin from British Sources:* logeion.uchicago.edu/lexidium

British History Online, 'Parliament Rolls of Medieval England': www.british-history.ac.uk/no-series/parliament-rolls-medieval

The National Archives, 'Palaeography Tutorial': www.nationalarchives.gov.uk/palaeography

University of Cambridge, Faculty of English, 'English Handwriting 1500–1700: An Online Course': www.english.cam.ac.uk/ceres/ehoc

University of Houston, 'Anglo-American Legal Tradition': aalt.law.uh.edu

University of Nottingham, 'Manuscripts and Special Collections': www.nottingham.ac.uk/manuscriptsandspecialcollections